SWEET SUCCESS

SWEET SUCCESS

DAVID K. SWEET, PH.D.

© Copyright 2020—David K. Sweet

All rights reserved. This book is protected by the copyright laws of the United States of America. No part of this publication may be reproduced, stored in or introduced into a retrieval system, or transmitted, in any form or by any means (electronic, mechanical, photocopying, recording or otherwise), without the prior written permission of the publisher. For permissions requests, contact the publisher, addressed "Attention: Permissions Coordinator," at the address below.

Published and distributed by:
SOUND WISDOM
P.O. Box 310
Shippensburg, PA 17257-0310
717-530-2122
info@soundwisdom.com
www.soundwisdom.com

While efforts have been made to verify information contained in this publication, neither the author nor the publisher assumes any responsibility for errors, inaccuracies, or omissions. While this publication is chock-full of useful, practical information; it is not intended to be legal or accounting advice. All readers are advised to seek competent lawyers and accountants to follow laws and regulations that may apply to specific situations. The reader of this publication assumes responsibility for the use of the information. The author and publisher assume no responsibility or liability whatsoever on the behalf of the reader of this publication.

The scanning, uploading and distribution of this publication via the Internet or via any other means without the permission of the publisher is illegal and punishable by law. Please purchase only authorized editions and do not participate in or encourage piracy of copyrightable materials.

Cover designed by Eileen Rockwell
Interior designed by Susan Ramundo

ISBN 13 TP: 978-1-64095-191-4
ISBN 13 eBook: 978-1-64095-192-1

For Worldwide Distribution, Printed in the U.S.A.
1 2 3 4 5 6 7 8 / 24 23 22 21 20

> Wealth does not bring about *arête* (excellence).
> *Arête* brings about wealth…and all other public
> and private blessings for humans.
>
> —Socrates, *Apology*

> Let us carefully observe those good qualities wherein
> our enemies excel us and endeavor to excel them,
> by avoiding what is faulty, and imitating
> what is excellent in them.
>
> —Plutarch, *Parallel Lives*

> Let us go then, you and I,
> When the evening is spread out against the sky
> Like a patient etherized upon a table;
> Let us go, through certain half-deserted streets,
> The muttering retreats
> Of restless nights in one-night cheap hotels
> And sawdust restaurants with oyster-shells:
> Streets that follow like a tedious argument
> Of insidious intent
> To lead you to an overwhelming question…
> Oh, do not ask, "What is it?"
> Let us go and make our visit.
>
> —T.S. Eliot, "The Love Song of J. Alfred Prufrock"

> This is going to be #epic!
>
> —Simon Jelfs

CONTENTS

#Sweet Success	11
#Commonplace Book	19
#Love to Do	26
#Exercise	29
#Childhood	31
#Persistence	33
#Fun	36
#Parents	41
#Positivity	45
#Amateur	48
#Letters	52
#Enthusiasm	54
#Body #Mind #Spirit	58
#Age 10	63
#When I'm 64	66
#Time Flies	68
#Let Them Eat Cake	71
#Reading	74
#Cooking	82
#Meditating	84

#Teachers	87
#Dreaming	91
#Goals #Promises #Vision	94
#Next Right Answer	99
#Intention	102
#Choices	105
#Education	109
#Dressing Up	113
#Memory	116
#Biographies	122
#Aesthetic	126
#Mistakes	129
#Greetings	133
#Walking	135
#Names	137
#Poetry	140
#Arête	145
#1%	150
#Eulogy	153
#Answers	157
#Aliens	160
#What If	163
#Gardening	165

#Angel's Advocate	168
#Humor	170
#Innocents Abroad	173
#Astronaut	175
#Pearly Whites	179
#Ideas	181
#Silence	183
#News	186
#Travel	189
#Feng Shui	191
#Liberal Arts	194
#Pics	199
#Choice	202
#Intuition	205
#Teaching	208
#Favorite Weapon	210
Serve Up Your Own Helping of #Sweet Success	215
#Sweet Success Books	217
#About the Author	223

#SWEET SUCCESS

So there I am, in my thirties, overweight, out of shape, poor, and needing to reinvent myself. I started to run. Growing up, I had done very little sports. In grade school, I hated judo because they kept throwing me to the ground and messing up my *dogi*. Baseball and soccer both frightened me as I feared the ball. I did a bit of Tae Kwon Do and in high school was interested in cross-country cycling until my bike was stolen. I was a nerd who found refuge in books and writing.

In 1998, I moved to Tokyo with my family and, to feed them, started out in sales, which I greatly enjoyed. Our company felt that being healthy promoted better sales, so I started running. After all, it gave me a chance to be alone a bit—we lived in a very small Japanese apartment. I also felt running was inherently a mental exercise; all I needed to do to run a marathon was create a program, follow it daily, and have the fortitude and persistence to complete the program. In short, I needed to train regularly more than anyone else. I found the process challenging, yet enjoyable. After my first marathon, I was hooked. I started to run all the time and loved marathons and then ultra-marathons. I became a self-proclaimed runaholic.

Sweet Success is similar in construction. I wanted a way to grow, learn, and develop both personally and professionally. I've never really thought about "work-life" balance; I've only considered everything "life." After all, when I walk into the office, my life doesn't cease. When I walk into my home, I still consider parts of my job. It was all part of me and my life.

Sweet Success is put together like a running program to work on the *arête*, excellence, of your physical, mental, and spiritual life. The selections have been blended so that things are mixed up a bit to keep it interesting.

In marathon training, I practice a variety of runs—some long, some short, some fast, some slow. Rather than a boring 10-kilometer run every day, it's more interesting to have variety—for example, some time at the track, a long 30-kilometer run, and a fast 14K tempo run.

Here too, some of the essays will have different themes, introducing you to new ideas, reinforcing others, and challenging how you currently live your life. Some of the ideas you'll already do. For example, as a runner I know how to run, but I can improve on my pacing. In this book, you'll find some nutrition ideas, which you may already know. Great! Other points on idea generation may be new to you. I would challenge you that those will be the ones that will give you more growth and open unknown doors for you.

I'm inviting you to join me in a few inspired ideas that have helped me in life. This is a casual affair with a friend to chat about everything from health to memory, from your childhood to old age. Not as sophisticated as Marcus Aurelius, but hopefully born from the same Stoic vein, and also mixed in with a healthy amount of Walt Whitman.

Here we are, and we can relax as among friends and slip off our shoes. We can sit down to a casual lunch under a tree and chat about life. Let the cool breeze blow over the tops of our feet—you there and me here. If you're lucky, you'll have your feet on soft grass or, even more luscious, wading in a warm pool. Maybe your toes will feel the dirt or sand. I confess that I'm inside with a soft rug under my feet, but it's fuzzy and soft to the touch.

And here, on the page, across time and space, we can exchange our thoughts—barefoot, relaxed, suspending closure and open to new ideas, exploring together what life is about and sharing the best that the universe has to offer.

PERFORMANCE IMPROVEMENT

We will explore performance improvement. I'll share with you some ideas and personal views and stories rather than pedantic absolutes or dogmatic systems. We are searching for a natural, organic approach that fits you rather than a one-size generic answer.

Because the writing is personal in nature, it is also an autobiography of sorts. There are stories of mentors who have given me life lessons and lessons I'm still trying to unravel. Hopefully, you'll find inspiration and a few "ah-has" in the essays and the exercises.

Inspiration is a noun that means "being mentally stimulated to do or feel something." Synonyms for the word are guiding light, creativity, and bright idea. If we follow the etymology of the word, you will find it in Middle English meaning "in the sense." I love that, because when we are out of flow of the world, we are generally *out* of our senses, versus *into* our senses. We are moving here or there, trying to get something done, moving fast, multitasking, reacting, and forgetting our senses.

In contrast, when we are in our sense, we are in ourselves, but not focused on ourselves; we are focused on something outside of us and how it relates to us. To dive into the spiritual and philosophical for a moment, it is *yang* and *yin*, active and receiving from an external force or energy. It is the subject and object and the awareness of the two and the process of the awareness.

As we follow the etymology further back, past the Old French to the Latin, the word changes into a verb, and the much more common history of the word meaning to "breathe into from a divine or supernatural being." Again, it is an awareness, but not of ourselves, not "self-awareness" but an awareness of the other. In this case, the divine. Our *arête*, that state of potential excellence, is in each of us, and it's our responsibility in life to release it.

ARÊTE

Arête comes from the Greek, and like many words from that very rich language, defies direct translation. The easiest concept is "excellence," especially in body and mind. When looking at Homer and the warriors of *The Iliad*, they were striving for *arête* in strength and bravery. In Plato, we find *arête* around the ideas of virtue, rather than strength. In Paul's letter to the Philippians, he follows the Greek idea and summarizes *arête* perfectly:

> *Finally, brothers, whatever is true, whatever is honorable, whatever is just, whatever is pure, whatever is lovely,*

> *whatever is commendable, if there is any* **excellence** *[arête], if there is anything worthy of praise, think about these things* (Philippians 4:8).

At the philosophical heart of this book, if I were to sum it up in one word, would be *arête*. In your own path to success, I want to assist you to live a life of *arête*—to strive for excellence, expect happiness, and accomplish something new and different, like paint or write a better email or run a faster marathon. I want you to find a bit of spice and flavor in your life.

Arête follows a humanist curiosity of what we've done as a human and a belief in what we can still accomplish. We are born an animal, a *homo sapiens*, and each of us needs to progress into being a human—moving from just an animal with opposable thumbs who collects the most sticks in the best cave, or in our modern day collection of money and the creature comforts of home and food and Netflix, into something greater that creates, develops, and helps the human race progress.

Many animal rights people I meet like animals better than people and have greater faith in dolphins or the speech of an orangutan than in that of their neighbor. I'm not here to belittle the animal kingdom; however, at the time of this writing, humans are the smartest, most creative, and most adaptive animals in the universe that I'm aware of. Nothing else on the planet is able to do—for better or worse—what humans can.

In addition, no intelligent alien life has been found. I've not seen a ghost or a being from another dimension. And as smart as I believe a poodle is or as exceptionally intelligent a dolphin or any other animal on this planet may be, I've yet to see anything but a human compose anything as gorgeous as Mozart's *Figaro* or paint anything as sublime as the Sistine Chapel or write anything as stirring as *War and Peace.*

POTENTIAL

You, however, have that potential. From here on a tiny blue rock in the Milky Way, you are unique like no other. In all the history of this Earth and—as mentioned, as of this writing—of the universe, there has never been and perhaps never again will be *you.* You with your inimitable makeup of experiences, talent, and personality. This makes you valuable to the whole human race. You carry part of our human collective, embodying the best (and, of course sometimes, as world leaders often prove, the worst) of human capabilities.

You have the potential to create, inspire, evolve, and grow beyond our current limited beliefs. I'll say, as Uncle Ben said to Peter Parker, with great power comes great responsibility. What we currently do to live on this planet is often negligent, harmful, disgraceful, and selfish. The mass production, manufacturing, and torturing of cattle and chickens is an abomination. We constantly pollute the oceans and sky and are irresponsibly destroying the forests. I understand the trade-offs and nothing is as easy as it seems. What I believe, however, is that more creative, smarter, engaged people sharing will help the humanist cause, which in turn will help the planet.

To do this, I want our time together to inspire you to create, think, observe, relax, design, and celebrate life so that you can improve your life and break free from whatever is holding you back. By doing this, you can in turn inspire others to do the same. And together, we can all sit down, relax and chat, and enjoy successful lives.

Some special people have helped me along in this path. First, Francisco Betancourt, who inspired me on this project and continues to inspire. "Inspire" comes from the Latin, meaning to "breathe into," usually from the divine that imparts truth and ideas to another. That describes Francisco and his invaluable contribution and influence.

Thank you to Ashley Harvey and Benjamin Martin for their valued input, perceptive insights, and kind guidance.

Simon Jelfs is definitely #epic, and I thank him for the editing, comments, and encouragement. Also a huge thanks to Simon for getting me off my butt and into running those many moons ago.

A cheers and toast to Anthony Trotter for his praise, inspiration, laughter, and editing.

A colossal thank you to Bob Poulson for his close reading and editing of the manuscript.

To David Wildasin and his team at Sound Wisdom who have always been supportive and kind.

Last, and definitely the most important, my family. My cherished wife, Tomoko, who constantly supports, encourages, and improves me. I love her dearly. My two sons, Reili and Tetsia, who have grown to be fine men who inspire me to be a better person.

And my parents who have been the best models a person could hope for.

May everyone have such wonderful people to surround themselves with and to share a sweet and successful life.

David Sweet
Tokyo, May 2019

#COMMONPLACE BOOK

A Commonplace Book originates from the categorizing and taking down of notes from what one reads—capturing quotes, images, and ideas. In contrast to a chronological journal or diary, a commonplace book is categorical. John Locke wrote a book on how to keep a commonplace book, and writers like John Milton and Virginia Woolf organized their thoughts into such notebooks. Harvard has photographs of commonplaces in a variety of languages dating back to the 16th century. Sometimes commonplaces will contain quotes, recipes, measurements, formulas, pictures, and other interesting scraps of memorabilia.

Like Aaron Copland's *Fanfare for the Common Man*, the word "common" made me feel that such a book would involve the ordinary, easy, and casual jotting down of information. Everyone could devise a commonplace book—an inclusive book that anyone could write and that contains anything and everything. I took the meaning far from just note taking. A commonplace book, I imagined, constructed an entrance ramp to the most democratic of entrances into thought, encompassing the common daily sights, sounds, observations, and impressions of the everyday: ladybugs on a breakfast plate near the toast, the smell of diesel fuel from a bus on a cold winter morning, the sound of snow crunching under feet, the monumental complaints of the day, a shiver from a brisk north wind in November, a complaint about how my coworker whistles out of tune, the calico cat next door, the green glass jar in the shop window, and a quote by W. Somerset Maugham. Nothing too important, but just little items that captured the attention.

Of course, the commonplace book would also capture the heaviest of world changing ideas, thoughts, plans, lists of creative endeavors, sketches for how to build a deck in the backyard, poems of death and love, lyrics of a song, or fragments of ideas for a letter to a lover.

In contrast to the commonplace, the word "journal" sounds serious and stuffy. We keep a journal the way that one "keeps" a pet, with some haughty connotations formed by published journals like *The Wall Street Journal*, *The Journal of Administrative Science*, or more extensive research-based journals like *The Journal of Investigative Dermatology*. A journal is for something important.

Like a commonplace book, a journal may be a doorway, but it feels less accessible. Perhaps an automatic door where anyone can enter, but engineered with a stairway leading up to the door. Attired in a black turtleneck sweater, opening a Moleskine notebook qualifies for a good journal—preferably unlined, with a few of the pages dog-eared. The observations of the day, sketches perhaps taken from the Tate Gallery, a sonnet or two, and the outline for the latest novel. No pages for hamburger recipes, jokes about hamsters, or Japanese vocabulary learned from the restaurant owner down the street.

Personally, I dreamed of having a commonplace that looked like the notebook carried by Indiana Jones in *Raiders of the Lost Ark*—tattered, worn, with maps, sketches, diagrams, and secrets written in code. Or da Vinci's notebook with drawings, cartoons, and elaborate observations of dissections, wings of birds, and flowing wind and waves. Maybe even a journal like that of Hendrik van Loon, with beautifully written passages and simple sketches describing George Washington crossing the Delaware with his troops for a surprise attack on that cold Christmas morning of 1776. Of course, there would also be a plethora of delightful aphorisms, deep humanistic insights, philosophical whims, several silly sketches from our office, and many off-color jokes. If drawing a humorous penis was good enough for Leonardo da Vinci, it's good enough for me, by golly.

Then in my dream, after I had long been dead and buried, all my tattered commonplace books would be found by some future collegiate Freudian scholar writing her or his master's thesis, poring ceaselessly over the pages, searching for some deep insights. Or perhaps my progeny would seek insights into their mysterious and quirky grandfather or great uncle, to find how he agonized over money or deeply loved his wife. The gentle secrets of his childhood might be revealed and occasionally, a sentence or two might inspire them. I wanted to fade into history while my commonplace books proudly orate like the replicant, Roy Batty, in *Blade Runner*:

> I've seen things you people wouldn't believe. Attack ships on fire off the shoulder of Orion. I watched C-beams glitter in the dark near the Tannhäuser Gate. All those moments will be lost in time, like tears in rain. Time to die.

Then there are diaries. Lovely little things, diaries. I picture Louisa May Alcott dressed in black lace, sitting at her writing table with her bonnet to the side as she selects the images from her daily life, the weather and the scone she had for breakfast with a tad of marmalade recorded in the gentle, rounded letters. In a diary, complaints about the cold slip in nicely next to notes about a stranger who visited in his silk hat and calf-skin gloves that he removed and then lovingly caressed his brown, handsome mustache.

Or maybe, a diary could conceal the facts of the day, the implied urges of the writer, which in turn give future Freudians stacks of research to sift through. Or maybe a diary is a bit more whimsical, kept on the bedside where sex and intrigue are recorded. Something Bridget Jones would be proud of.

Personally, I got my first diary when I was seven or eight years of age. It was a red velvet book that snapped shut with a metal button. On the cover was written in gold, "Diary." Inside, there was a "19___" where the year could be handwritten in, along with the month and day. Then I could write along the gold lined paper with my favorite writing instrument, which at the time was a BIC four-color pen. It housed green, black, blue, and red ink. I fearlessly used all four colors, sometimes in the same entry. The letter shapes are shaky—the early attempts at cursive writing by someone who has just learned how to connect all the letters together.

One day I snuck into Mom's bedroom, and on her nightstand found her own diary or journal. I opened it. Her words were scribbled in black felt pen. Her letters were round, neat, easy for my elementary school learning to scan. I remember casually glancing over the words only searching for one thing—my name. I ignored the rest. Here and there were references to me and I could learn about myself, my mother's secret thoughts about me. Then I found something that shocked me. She had been reading my diary. I slammed the book shut. I wanted to confront her; but because I was reading her journal, there was no real way for me to bring it up. It was quite a conundrum, so I kept my secret; and whenever I wrote, guarded my thoughts. I had discovered the importance of having a reading audience, even when we believed we were writing only for ourselves.

Even now, the connotation of diary still holds many secrets.

Now, I sit in my office typing on my Mac. I found a great little app called "Day One," where I can scribble down an entry—my electronic commonplace book that works on my mobile phone and tablet. Though it looks like I'm texting or responding to email, in reality I'm jotting down scenes and thoughts, ideas and dreams. Thirty years ago, I carried a pocket notebook and tiny ballpoint pen the size of a toothpick around with me everywhere. With the joys of technology, it's much easier to jot down ideas anywhere and anytime. With a computer or tablet, I can type or dictate, then cut and paste into a blog, essay, poem, or story.

I had a writing friend who told me that writing on paper is writing with earth and stone (paper and pen) versus writing on the computer, which is writing with light. The nature of the tools allows for different dynamics. Myself, I compose stories with the computer. Poetry and essays, I always do my first draft in pen and paper. There are no hard or fast rules, though, and I change with my interests. I'm in a transition shifting back into using notebooks more and more—going analog.

In primary school I wrote a diary, and then I graduated to a journal. In university, I found Julia Cameron's *Morning Pages*—three pages of longhand. I was religious in writing every morning. I would roll out of bed, regardless of the time or temperature, and write. If I had to take an early plane at 6:30 a.m., I would wake at 4:30 to write. I wanted to record dreams, feel in flow, and experience synchronicity. Then I found Natalie Goldberg's *Writing Down the Bones*. She described writing like meditation, thoughts flowing on the page. Next, came Stephen King's idea from his excellent book, *On Writing*, where writing is "telepathy, of course." He explains how a writer in his time and place can connect to the reader in her time and place. Walt Whitman too believed he was connecting with the reader. I too believe the same and am happy to connect with you now. Are you still barefoot?

All these combine for me into a friendly Commonplace Book, or CB for short. A CB is a friendly, casual place to relax, to scribble, journal, record events, meditate, and connect to our future selves. The notebooks are random, messy, and comfortable like an old pair of jeans, a warm sweater, or favorite pajamas. The majority of the words scribbled are messy and often illegible. Once in a while, a good idea shows up, but not generally. It doesn't need to. This is a place to process and relax. Ideas may be lights in the night sky, but there's no need to expect planets or moons. Mainly, it's gibberish, and that's groovy. Just common. Just a commonplace for a common person, just as the stars are common. It is always good to remember that each star is a sun's chance to shine, just as each common word and thought is a unique chance for us to capture and realize our life and share our thoughts. The point, though, is to take those common ideas, and then create a spectacular life with extraordinary works.

#SWEET SUCCESS: Go buy a notebook. Something easy, comfortable. I change mine all the time. Sometimes it's a simple spiral notebook. Other times, I splurge for a fancy cover. I recently bought an expensive Moleskine because it was blue velvet and had a Rolling Stones tongue on it. I like to have something large enough to capture ideas or draw, but small enough that I can carry it if needed. My favorite is a very inexpensive A5 size (210 mm × 297 mm or 8 in. × 11 in.) notebook. Try several and see what works. Keep it simple.

#LOVE TO DO

Your life is unique, special, and one of a kind; so far in all of human exploration, with Voyager moving out past Pluto into the Kuiper belt and beyond, with telescopes penetrating the farthest galaxies within the universe, more and more stars are being discovered. Each star is a sun. Around those suns are other worlds with some of the planets like our humble blue Earth. If we imagine these fantastic planets with other people, maybe some of them like our Earth, with more than 7 billion people, their own histories that stretch back thousands of years with countless other people, we can begin to think of how many possibilities there are in the universe.

However, with all those possibilities, *there has never been, nor ever will be, another **you***. You are the only person with your unique DNA, experiences, and living right here and right now. You are the only chance that the universe will ever have of experiencing *you*. This is your chance to find what you love and do that.

For some reason, in our daily lives it's easy to get busy and forget about the things we love to do. You think you love to binge on Netflix, read the newspaper, chat with your neighbor, coach soccer practice, have a beer while watching the Patriots game, or upload pictures to Facebook. However, when you begin to list these items, you start to evaluate and compare with others on the list. You weigh the most important and start to ask questions:

- Was this really what I *love* to do?

- Was this only something I *like* doing?

- Is it something my spouse or partner or friend likes doing and I just follow along?

- When I do this activity, am I smiling?

You live once. You never know how long that life might be. It's like the scene in *Meet Joe Black*, when a young man, played by Brad Pitt, has just finished having a coffee with the lovely Susan Parrish, played by Claire Forlani. It's a first meeting, love at first sight, where the "lightning could strike." They part, missing each other's backward glances. Then Pitt, star-crossed and absent-minded, crosses the street and is honked at. From the other direction he is hit by two cars and instantly killed.

Though this is fiction, there are too many times in daily life when a person is swept away in a breath. This exercise isn't here to make you feel depressed or sad, but to give you a chance to evaluate what is important in your life and then again enjoy the activities that really matter to you.

#SWEET SUCCESS: Get out your new CB and write a list of 25 things you love to do. This is a personal list with no wrong answers. And yes, binging on Netflix can be on that list! So too might be listening to the Cocteau Twins, roller-blading with a friend, making an enchilada dinner, potting a plant, riding a horse, laying in the grass and watching clouds pass by, watching the stars, writing poetry, hot air ballooning, origami, eating chocolate ice cream with a coworker, digging your toes deep in the sands of the nearest beach, learning to play drums, or visiting a second-hand furniture shop downtown. Whatever it is, write it down.

Next to each of these, place the date when you last did it. Now select one of them and make a commitment to do it within the week. Life is too short not to do the things you love. If you loved doing them once, maybe they are worth doing again.

#EXERCISE

Our present time, even with all its shortcomings, is mindbogglingly outstanding—more people on the planet can live better, healthier, and longer than at any other time in history. The vehicle you have to move you around this quality life is your body, and you must care for it to maintain a long, productive life. If your body goes, it becomes increasingly difficult to think, create, and dive into new endeavors that enhance your own life and the lives of people around you. For that reason, I consider this section one of the most important.

I'm not a natural athlete and literally stayed as far away from exercise as humanly possible until my thirties. As a kid, I hated sports. I had terrible hand-eye coordination. For team sports, like soccer and baseball, I got nervous and made mistakes. Gym class was even worse, being slow, awkward, and weak. On sports day, I got the puke-green ribbon for "Good Sportsmanship."

When I was in my mid-thirties, I had started to bulge a bit around my midriff; in other words, I was fat. I didn't think anything of it, as appearance was unimportant to me. However, I had just started a new job in sales. Energy, mental toughness, and appearance were all important in the job and the management team thought wellness was important. As a manager, I needed to lead by example, so I started running.

My first day out, I jogged five minutes, walked five, and finished with a plodding five-minute jog before collapsing—pale and exhausted, but happy. I found running suited me as coordination and teams didn't matter. I just needed persistent, consistent practice. Now I run marathons and ultra-marathons for the sheer joy of it—much to the surprise of those who knew me growing up, including myself.

I tell this story because I believe that if I can do it, literally anyone can do it. I believe that consistent exercise will greatly boost your energy and the ideas available to you. Elevating your heart rate for twenty-five minutes for a minimum of three times a week, and preferably five times a week, will help you strengthen your heart and sleep better. Try more exercise until you find something that interests you.

For me, it turned out to be running, karate, and yoga. You might try to find a group or may wish to go it alone. Try walking—absolutely one of the best things for your mind and body, which is why I devote a section to it. Or if you prefer, wall climbing, jumping rope, salsa dancing, weight lifting, biking, Pilates, hip-hop dancing, elliptical or rowing machines, or a brisk hike. Aerobic exercise gets oxygen to your brain, making you think well. It also builds endorphins, a natural high, making you happier. You need not compete nor ever be a superstar athlete. What I'm advocating is good maintenance of your health that helps you create and enjoy your life for as long as possible.

#SWEET SUCCESS: Commit to exercise three times this week. It can be as simple as a brisk walk. Do something that will raise your heartbeat.

#CHILDHOOD

This section asks you to remember your childhood. Like all good stories, let's begin with a place—the place that shapes our character, you! Place is important. It shapes our ideas and behaviors. Rivers and fertile valleys lead to farming rather than hunting. Greek city-state democracy was shaped by its islands, Venice by its lagoons, the United States by its vast, open expanse.

Where you were raised, especially your room where you spent time playing and sleeping, shapes some of who you became. The memories there have faded, but hover in a haze, like a dream. When you tap into this region of your memory, you start to explore a creative, imaginative side of yourself. This imaginative side is chock-full of emotions and sensory experiences, once forgotten and then resurfaced. Memories are powerful. They sometimes keep emotions hidden like trinkets placed on a high shelf. When you start to explore, you find that you remember more and more and emotions will come back to you.

When you dive back into your childhood memories, you can start to think about where you slept, the furniture in your house and room, books, toys. Many of the memories are of "firsts" from your life. There is a sense of newness and wonder. Memories are powerful tools to link to our ability to visualize and in turn, be creative. Memories are like dreams. We are able to nearly touch them. By diving back into your childhood and looking around, you find a tool that will help you visualize for every part of your life.

#SWEET SUCCESS: Pull out your commonplace book and describe the first room you remember as a child. Maybe you'll start by walking through the door. Describe what you see and where it was placed. Use all your senses—in addition to sight, describe how things feel, smell, taste, and sound. What do you remember? What was your favorite thing about this room? What was your favorite memory? What can you take from here and incorporate into your life now?

Some of the memories may be sad; keep writing and push through writing about why you're sad. If they make you laugh, keep writing and describe why you're laughing. This is a chance to explore and dive deep into childhood, memories, and feelings. By putting words around the description, even if it isn't the precise word or description, that's okay. The point is the process of writing about the memories and feelings and invigorating yourself with old feelings that you may have forgotten and what caused them.

#PERSISTENCE

I believe that profound changes take time. Get rich quick, 11 steps to success, 30 days to health, and 10 days to riches only touch the surface. I believe that it's consistent, small actions over the long haul that make the greatest changes. For me, I've read many of these books on how to make transformational changes in my workweek, super time management, mental mindsets, positive attitudes, and any other number of self-help books. But they haven't had any lasting, significant impacts that worked for my life, my family, and me.

I have been able to make changes, grow, and succeed in certain endeavors in my life—happy family life, successful in my professional field, educated, and gone from fat to fit. I'm not winning the Nobel Prize or the Olympics, but life is good.

What I've accomplished has been mainly through that thing that people call "hard work." What it really was though is taking small actions consistently. Some people will say it is steps, but I've not followed too many steps; rather, I had a vision, read lots of books, listened to lots of people, and then consistently implemented what I learned. I turned off the television and restricted my social media (how easy is it to lose hours watching YouTube videos!). I was able to work a full-time job and earn a doctorate because I enjoyed what I studied and knew that the investment in my knowledge would help enrich my life. There was no guarantee it would do anything for my bank account, but that seems to take care of itself.

I also have experimented and run into a lot of dead-ends. In publishing, like most authors, I've collected a great many rejection slips. I've sat down to literally hundreds of interviews without receiving a job offer. And as of the time of this writing, I'm still trying to reach that mystical sub-3-hour marathon.

What makes life changes possible is persistence and staying power. One of my friends posted the famous Calvin Coolidge quote in our office:

> Nothing in this world can take the place of persistence. Talent will not: nothing is more common than unsuccessful men with talent. Genius will not: unrewarded genius is almost a proverb. Education will not: the world is full of educated derelicts. Persistence and determination alone are omnipotent.

As mentioned, when I was in elementary school, my very athletic father put me first in baseball and later in soccer. My hand-eye coordination was appalling and I was terrified of being hit by the ball in both sports. I was basically a failure in sports. Then into my thirties, with a growing family and working long hours, I had grown fat. I started running. In a few short months, I started to run races, and in a year I was running over five marathons a year. What I had found was that persistence could win a race—five days running five kilometers was better than one day of 25 kilometers or two days of 12.5 kilometers.

#PERSISTENCE

This started to carry through to everything in my life. I found that with tenacity and persistence, I could gain a level of proficiency in everything I tried. I may not be a natural salesperson, but knowing that I needed to do a certain number of calls and meetings made it easier to figure out my actions. The same held true for my family relationships—if I consistently spent time with my wife and kids instead of television, the relationships blossomed. And with writing, I kept putting words to paper and had the books grew.

Consistent persistence on small things has had the greatest impact on every aspect of my life. In contrast, all the get rich, get smart, do anything better, faster methods out there in the world have not worked for me. I've tried them. And have given them a good shot with considerable effort. However, what has worked for me was just taking the time and putting in the effort, day after day, and having fun doing it.

#SWEET SUCCESS: In your CB, write for ten minutes about something you've done persistently. This could be your constant effort to learn how to bake the perfect chocolate cake, to master watercolors, learn accounting, raise a child, play an instrument, or learn the lyrics to every Beatles song. Now stretch for a minute, walk around your chair, sit down and write for another ten minutes; write about things you would like to improve in your life. After you're done, reread what you've written. Do you see anything that you could do constantly to improve? Commit to put one thing into practice.

#FUN

Having fun is subjective. Some people find painting models fun. Others like to play with pictures on their computer. Some write exceptional blogs. Others can bounce a soccer ball on their feet hundreds of times. I know people who can bake and others who draw comics. One guy I know can play the banjo. For me, I love to run hundreds of kilometers a month.

In all these examples, "fun" does not necessarily equate with "easy." Fun contains a certain degree of mastery. Mastery comes from consistent dedication to a process until effort changes into something easier, but still with a new level of difficulty.

For example, when I go to the pool, I flop down the lane, splashing, huffing and puffing, and gulping down water like a college student gulps down beer. I long to have the smooth breaststroke, the seamlessly effortless gliding that comes from hundreds of hours of practice. Within that "seamless, effortless" process, however, there is a new level of master; for example, it could be speed or distance. For me, I try to survive; for the experts, they are mastering their skills.

All endeavors have this learning curve toward mastery. They say it takes ten thousand hours or ten years to reach mastery of a craft. To progress from the novice to the expert comes from the persistence mentioned in the previous section. It's why musicians play scales, painters sketch, writers journal, and runners hit the track.

The subtle joys of practice make the mastery worthwhile. Many of us suffered through piano lessons when we were young. We dreaded the practice and the boredom of scales. To see the chance to move from Hot Cross Buns to Mozart in a month was beyond comprehension. So we quit.

If you are working on mastering a new task where you need to practice—be it tennis, algebra, or cold calling—break down the process into smaller units that you can master and then celebrate when the parts begin to come together. Look for quick wins.

One of the reasons I loved doing karate was the different belt levels where I could move from white to gold, then green, and so on. The higher up in belt ranking, the further in the back of the class I stood. As I practiced from the back of the class, I could also watch the students with the lower belts practice. A black belt sensei, or teacher, would correct the lower belts, but as an upper level student, I could see the correction and would self-correct. This created an environment of self-teaching, self-correction, self-awareness, and a process toward mastery while saving face. Such a process made the challenge achievable and the learning fun.

In the United States in the 19th century, for one-room schoolhouses it was often necessary for the older students to assist the teacher in teaching the younger students. Today, we see this in universities. The ability to teach also helps to provide mastery and growth and helps to bring joy to the process. This joy, with small incremental progress, makes mastery come within reach.

#SWEET SUCCESS: In your life now, what tasks do you dread doing? Jot down some ways to make them fun.

For example, if you're in sales and dread making cold calls, jot down ten ways to make it fun:

1. Make a time to cold call with other salespeople.

2. Try to use the word "sparkling" in a conversation. Then try to fit the word "Zimbabwe" into the conversation (the lateral thinking required makes the call interesting).

3. Give yourself a small treat after five successful connects.

4. Walk around while calling.

5. Make some cold calls out in the park.

6. Within your ten calls, make sure one of the calls is to your grandmother (cold calls, like calling your grandma, may not be something you want to do, but afterwards you feel really good—thanks for this one, Anthony Trotter!).

7. Aim to ask three open-ended questions in the call.

8. Race to finish a certain number of connects within a certain amount of time.

9. Stand on the desk and make five calls (thanks Ray Dile, sales mentor, who taught me the brilliance of this one).

Or maybe you dread cleaning your home or workspace:

1. Play some uplifting music.

2. Buy something for your place and then clean so you have a nice spot to put it.

3. Invite a friend to help.

4. Invite a friend over afterward…motivating you to clean.

5. Outsource it—hire a friend, family member, or service.

6. Make a YouTube video on how you clean your room quickly.

7. Instagram the process.

8. Look for five things you can give to charity as you clean.

9. Decide you don't mind it dirty and just ignore the whole damn thing and go to a movie.

10. See how much you can clean in ten minutes. Set your timer. Go!

Now find some things that you'd like to make more fun in your life. Try anniversary dinners, birthday parties, studying for exams, sex, cooking, writing a report, going to the dentist, or painting a portrait. Be creative, outlandish, politically incorrect, silly, and daring. Know that there isn't a wrong way, just a new way, which is fun.

#PARENTS

My mother, a Lutheran pastor, earned a doctorate and two masters degrees, so growing up I thought of her as a smart lady. She, and other women who felt the pressures of a glass ceiling holding them down, acquired the education to compete as a woman in a traditionally men-only profession. She did all this and was a hell of a great mom too.

After I was born, an old back injury acted up and she needed to have eighteen operations in twelve months or twelve surgeries in eighteen months. She was on so much medication at the time, she forgot which was which.

When I was five, I remember Dad bringing her home in a wheelchair. Her bed was put in the downstairs living room, as she couldn't walk; her bedroom and study on the second floor were out of the question. When I came home from school, I made her a peanut butter and jelly sandwich for lunch. The doctors said she would probably never walk again as she was missing some of the parts of her spine. But after rehab and pain and persistence, she started moving, walking, and even climbing the stairs. She then decided to go back to school. She also raised me in a very creative fashion.

Her recovery taught me to have a belief and faith and wonder in the universe. It also taught me that we have talents and we need to take care of them. The universe brings a great deal to the table. I'm not speaking here of any religion or spiritual belief, but that "There are more things in heaven and earth, Horatio, than are dreamt of in your philosophy," as says Shakespeare.

Mom taught me to listen to Beethoven's *Pastoral Symphony*, or *Symphony No. 6*, while waiting for the sunrise. After watching *The Music Man*, we took out pots and pans and we banged them, marching around the house as proud as Harold Hill and as noisy as any band.

One morning when I was in the fourth grade, she woke me up and said, "Would you like to stay home from school? I'll take you to see *Fantasia*. The movie will help you more in life than any day of school." And she did; and she was right.

She gave me Mark Twain, Robert Louis Stevenson, and Voltaire to read when I was in fourth grade. She made me write papers during summer break and we often walked up to the local lake and sat outside to read. Because money was a bit tight one summer, she snuck us into the local condominium, as there was a pool. She wanted to take me swimming, and no one expected a mother with a small boy to sneak in.

Because I was hyperactive, like most boys, she taught me to meditate, which is how she was controlling her back pain. Because I loved to put on costumes and sneak into her makeup, she entered me into a local drama class at the college she attended. I'll tell you more about that too. She taught me manners, how to waltz, and which fork to use when several were on the table.

This was the start of much of what I know, practice, and teach. Not that all my childhood was grand and Pollyanna. For me, fitting into school was difficult. What my parents taught me was that education was something that the parents were responsible for, not the schools, and she often said that 70 percent of education happens at home and only 30 percent in school—a good number for any parent to remember. She also taught me that learning was a community and one needs to develop that community in order to learn and grow.

She continually taught me to try new things and challenge the status quo. There is always a system for school, work, society, and community, and you play the game, make it through the system, but in the end you're responsible for your own life, thinking, action, and choices.

So there are two points to highlight for you. First, you're in control of your choices. You can choose to like or hate, frown or laugh, act or rest. You can choose not to choose. Life is a summation of the choices you make.

Second, education, real education, is a process that happens throughout life, especially when accompanied by great curiosity. Education consists of everything, not just one specialization. "Life is so rich and abundant with so much to learn, and we are born with talents to use," was the lesson she taught.

#SWEET SUCCESS: Take out your commonplace book and write about your parent or the person who raised you. Do this in a stream of consciousness—just write without stopping, not going back to correct spellings or punctuation or to worry about grammar. Just write as fast as your pen will take you. You're not trying to create an essay, memoir, or story, just get the ideas out of your head and onto the paper.

What stories do you remember? What has helped make you who you are? When did you laugh? What was crazy? What was educational? What was special? And what about this person made it unique for you?

#POSITIVITY

This section is based on a theory called the Sapir-Whorf hypothesis developed by linguists in the mid-20th century. In short, it says that your thoughts influence your decisions and actions. Of course, like all theories there is plenty of debate about how much words influence our reality, but in effect they do change how we live our lives.

Let's take a look at the negative and then what happens if put it into a positive, active voice.

NEGATIVE

- I don't want to get sick.
- I'm afraid of losing everything.
- I don't want you to leave.
- I don't want to work.
- I hate the rain.

POSITIVE

- I want to be healthy.
- I want to be rich.
- I want you to stay.
- I want to work my passion.
- I like being in the sun.

When you start to speak in the positive, you move forward. Positive language shifts toward the active. You control your surroundings. If life is a summation of your choices and you choose to be a victim, then the world controls you, your life, and your fate. You are a reckless, lackluster loser, controlled by the government or forces of nature or God or some other external force. The one benefit from this viewpoint is that you're not responsible; you're not to blame. And hey, who wouldn't like to live a blame-free life? We hate to be wrong.

What I'm saying here is that people really need to take charge of the direction of their lives and the energy that they push forward into the world. If you tell someone that you "love the rain" rather than that you "hate the rain," you are putting positive energy out there in the world. The rain doesn't change. You change. You are helping other people to move forward and smile and laugh. You are helping others to live a more positive world. You are loving life and moving forward.

Think to yourself, would you rather be around positive or negative people? We instinctively like happy and smiling people. Though sometimes it's challenging to put a positive spin on the world— you may have a sick child, have lost your job, have a cheating spouse, a gambling addiction, diabetes, or any number of challenges that plague us in life. You may have those times— and sometimes those times are years—when it is difficult to have a positive outlook. To buck those times, continue to speak in the positive.

Some things are certainly dreadful. If a spouse has cancer, it is a challenge to turn your thoughts into a decisive, positive direction. This takes strength and courage. We all know that we live on the razor's edge of oblivion, but to smile into the joy we have on this planet and to see the bright side of the day brings joyful energy to others. You sometimes do not know what is happening in their life, and your smile, your appreciation of rain, your ability to make someone else laugh can open the world for them and make their day a special place.

#SWEET SUCCESS: This week, eliminate the negative in this simple way: remove the word "not" and rephrase things in the positive. "I'd rather not go out" translates into, "I'd rather stay home." "I don't like him" could mean that you like to be around positive people. Look at this simple little word in your vocabulary and see how eliminating it can change your views and your reality. Once you know what you want, then you have some direction. If you lack direction, that's okay too. Start moving, flowing, and asking yourself, "What do I want?"

#AMATEUR

The etymology of *amateur* comes from the Latin, meaning "to love." When you think of doing something you love, there is a joy of practicing, losing yourself in the activity. The rest of the world fades away. Think of what it's like to spend the day out on the golf course when you're sinking a ball with ease or when you're drawing a picture and the whole afternoon passes by unaware. For some it may be preparing a meal for a friend the whole afternoon. For others, playing chess with a friend for hours. The common element is the focus on the process, not the outcome.

In schools and professions, there is a focus on outcome rather than process. We work toward a goal—a good grade, the almighty dollar, a sale, a KPI, a good performance report. In contrast, by focusing on the process and the practice of the process, you bring joy to the activity and seek to learn mastery of the craft.

Richard was leading a sales office that was floundering. "It's a really good market, we should be killing it." Instead, the team struggled to make meetings with prospective customers. Richard showed me the Key Performance Indicators (KPIs). "See, we are making the calls, but just not enough. The sales team fears rejection. Some of them are taking two hours to make ten simple calls."

"How can you make the process fun?" I asked.

"Well, I guess we could do a sales game. Competition always makes it fun. Maybe even throw in a prize, like a Starbucks voucher."

I met with Richard a month later and he was beaming. "There is a hum in the office. Everyone is on the phone, zooming in and out of meetings. We have added a couple more contests in the office. Some of the team like it, others don't. But what I notice is that there is much more care in the process." Richard pulls out a graph with the KPIs charted on them. "And look at this. Our KPIs are off the chart compared to the month before."

Stuck artists often have the same challenge as well. Vikki, who was working on a novel, felt she had hit a dead end. "I just don't know what to do next. Anyway, the chance of any agent or publisher buying the work is slim to none. I don't know. Maybe I'm not cut out for this."

Vikki was stuck on selling a novel that wasn't even written yet. We spoke about just focusing on the joy of writing, creating characters and scenes and weaving them together. She kept writing and when we met again, she was nearly finished. "It doesn't really matter if it sells or not," she told me. "It's been fun and a super learning experience. Looking forward to the next novel as well!"

Vikki too was learning to work out of love rather than outcome.

Being an amateur—whether in art, science, math, or some other field—used to be preferred. People learned a craft for pleasure rather than pay. There is a story that Charles Darwin wanted to go off to university to study science. His father was concerned that he would want to be a "professional." Before letting young Charles run off to university, he had to promise he would be an amateur—for the love of learning.

Some of us may find that we are amateur golfers; others, like myself, runners. If you wish, become an amateur photographer, pianist, writer, painter, or Ikebana enthusiast. The point is to find pleasure through mastering the discipline of process. Never worry that anyone will pat you on the back. Learn from Miles Davis: "Do not fear mistakes; there are none." The creative process is based on creating new, and sometimes we need to go through the bad to find the good in the creation. There are definitely times to learn musical scales, but sometimes you just need to hit the keys, wallow around in the sound, and try to pick out a tune by ear or make up your own music.

Whether or not it takes ten thousand hours (or ten years) or a lifetime to master a craft, it's time to get started.

#SWEET SUCCESS: Professionally allow yourself amateur status by focusing on the process rather than outcome. If you're an accountant, focus on the process of how you are putting together the budget. If you're in sales, look at the processes that you daily and weekly need to accomplish to make a sale: Which of the processes can you improve? Which of them can you make more interesting, fun, and enjoyable? Can you take your phone calls outside? Can you race against time and make a game of it?

#SWEET SUCCESS: Focus on a hobby and see what your process is there. If you cook from cookbooks, try a meal where you create your own dish. And look at some of the processes that you can learn, such as all the delightful cutting techniques and their names—julienne, bayonet, large dice, paysanne, and brunoise. The continued growth of just learning the terms will widen your abilities in the kitchen and may change how a meal tastes. You won't need to worry about ten thousand hours; you can focus on enjoying the process of learning.

#LETTERS

In this time of email and texting, we forget the power and *gravitas* of the humble, handwritten letter. It used to take time to send and receive a letter. For that reason, a bit more effort was involved in the crafting of it, though not much more time. Letters, the ancestor to that speedier email, still had a light, conversational tone. Some letters would be drafted and then rewritten, but more often than not, a letter was written out and mailed. The delete key was unavailable. What you wrote took you down the page. The casual speaking through words to a specific reader—an audience—gave writing a singular focus.

When composing formal types of writing, such as an essay, story, or poem, the author takes the time to contrive the stories and images or adds a great deal of logic to a formal argument. Grammar is perfectly laid down, form hammered into place, thoughts transverse like the continental railroad. In contrast, a letter allows the writer to meander, wander, and tangent, jumping from subject to subject. And in contrast to the journal or memoir, there is a definite audience for the writer. The person receiving the letter provides you with a context. Your writing tone, the words you choose, the anecdotes selected for your friend would be done one way, for your parents another, and yet a fan mail to a famous person another way.

In my life, letter writing has taken on a special place. After I met a Japanese girl at Neuschwanstein Castle in Germany, she and I became pen pals. Each month I would anticipate the arrival of a letter. I'd walk out to the mailbox, peek inside, longing to see a pink envelope. Then when it arrived, there was such joy in touching the paper with the floral pattern. I'd observe the twirl of her elegant handwriting, looking over each word. Soon, I would dash off a reply. The whole process would begin again and I would patiently have to wait for the next letter. Eight years passed this way until we met again. Then we fell in love and married.

Never underestimate the power of the written word and especially the importance of the handwritten letter.

#SWEET SUCCESS: Just for fun, write a letter to an eminent human. What would you tell someone like Alexander the Great or Shakespeare or Einstein or Gandhi or Catharine the Great or Hildegard of Bingen or Emily Dickinson about your day or life? Feel free to write to someone who is alive and send the letter. Who knows, maybe Michael Jordan, Mick Jagger, Larry King, Stephen King, Barack Obama, Gal Gadot, Oprah Winfrey, Malala Yousafzai, or Nicki Minaj will write back to you. Feel free to select anyone you like, be it a long-lost teacher or coach, a relative or parent. Or maybe someone from your list of the biographies you read and you would like to go back and ask them questions: What would seem important? What do you think they would say back? What questions would you ask? What answers can you anticipate?

Have fun with the exercise, realizing that unlike an actual letter or email, you don't need to send it—the only person who needs to read your letter is you.

#ENTHUSIASM

"Make every day a day of joy.
Dance, play, day and night…
Cherish the child who grasps your hand.
Let your wife rejoice in your bosom
For this is the fate of man."

—*The Epic of Gilgamesh*

I'm sitting at my desk and drinking coffee. It's bitter, but I sip it with intention to enjoy the taste, noticing the hint of honey and lime. I make the act special. Tasting my morning coffee as well as opening a new book, hugging my wife in the morning, and eating dinner with my sons all come with excitement and enthusiasm. Some days it is easier than others, but the sheer act of intention works to make an action important. Intent with enthusiasm opens joy for our lives. The word *enthusiasm* comes from the Greek word *enthous*, which means "possessed by a god, inspired." To come to an activity inspired makes the world a wonderful place.

American philosopher John Dewey wrote a book on aesthetics titled *Art as Experience* that nicely explains how we come to a work of art and experience it: the art has potential poured into it from the artist; we have our life experience poured into us. Combining the art and the viewing, the viewer creates an experience that is more than the two separate things. We can also lead our lives this way. If we come to an activity with the intent to have inspiration and enthusiasm, we are living the moment that is pregnant with joy. Literally we can breathe life into an activity.

Naturally, we breathe life into all our activities. Often, though, it is without consciousness. Still, the energy we bring does create that "experience." For example, if you walk into a room where people are sitting quietly, the energy of the room shifts. If you then begin to speak in a loud voice, people will look. If you laugh, perhaps people will smile. If you yell, people may fear. All this shifts the energy of the silent room. Our lives, though much more cluttered than an empty room, also have this flow of energy.

One of the oldest books in the world, the *I Ching* (or *The Book of Changes*), originally written around the time of Homer, presents the idea of working with the powers of yin and yang. Yin, the receptive; yang, the active. Of course, this is a gross simplification. But it helps us to understand that sometimes we move with life and are receptive (yin) and other times active (yang).

When I'm looking at a sunset, I am yin, receptive, absorbing all that I can of that moment and letting it act upon me, move me, create joy within me. When I'm running a marathon, in contrast, I'm active and literally trying to change the environment around me. Holding a child, I may be very yin in feeling the soft skin; teaching a child, I will be yang and explain, quiz, and check for understanding. Sometimes, listening to a good piece of music, I may let it wash over me, being totally receptive, and at other times, I will actively listen to the chords, repetitions, modulations, and interpretation in an active manner.

Rather than as nouns, I like to use yin and yang as verbs: sometimes you yin, sometimes you yang. When you yang, you're the active agent who creates the moment, who can really pour into the moment all the emotions of the universe.

And that's your choice—yang or yin? Which do you do? It need not be an ancient Chinese mystery, and there is no right answer. You can use such an idea in a much more practical, easy manner. You are an active agent or a passive agent. Within the pregnant moment, you chose to act or receive. Again, there is no correct answer, just the choice of how you live your life. Many of our entertainments, such as watching sports, surfing the Internet, television binging, and killing time on social media are all passive activities. In themselves, for a short relaxation, they are a welcome distraction from a hectic life, but overindulging throws our yang and yin balance out of order. In contrast, overworking, multi-tasking, excessive driven behaviors make us overactive and are just as destructive to a balanced life.

I'd be hypocritical if I said that we are looking for balance. As an entrepreneur and self-proclaimed runaholic, my life is anything but the Buddhist Middle Way. What I wish to give to you is the idea that there is a choice. Within the present, generate enthusiasm for the activity and decide to shape the moment or receive how the moment is presented and even both if applicable. The choice is yours. Having the intention and living in the moment to create it or to receive the creation opens a great variety of experience for you, building a life full of joy and rich experience.

#SWEET SUCCESS: Take out your CB and complete these questions:

- What five things do you do that waste your time?

- What five things do you yang/active that build rich experiences?

- What five things do you yin/passive that build rich experiences?

- What five things could you be doing more of in your life to build rich experiences?

#BODY #MIND #SPIRIT

This may come off as one of those "New Age" or pop-psychology ideas. Whenever I hear *body, mind, and spirit*, I get very, very nervous and want to run away as if a cult member was chasing me through the airport. But when I started putting all these ideas down on paper, I realized that the lowest common denominator was body, mind, and spirit.

So let's kick off our shoes, grab some lunch, and spend a bit of philosophical time together. I'll try to be as pragmatic as possible.

BODY: the body is what we live in. It is the earth of who we are. The body component is composed of the physical aspects and the environment in which that physical component was trained.

Our body is the capsule that allows us to do what we do—or, in some cases, hinders us from doing what we do. If we want to hike, draw, play piano, horseback ride, paint, or eat fine French pastries, we are enhanced or engaged by our senses and physical bodies. As a marathon runner, I have my body and my training; I train and make my legs and lungs stronger, but because I started training late in life, an opportunity to run in the Olympics probably isn't in the cards.

It might be easier for someone with long fingers to play the piano, someone with long legs to run, and someone with excellent eyesight to be a good pilot. In contrast, someone who is short may have challenges in basketball, someone color blind may abstain from painting, someone who lost a finger may shy away from the piano, and someone without a hand may skip playing baseball.

Along with the physical aspect, there is our environment. Your surroundings, people, and customs all helped to form you. If you were born near the equator, the opportunities to become a world-class figure skater, skier, and bobsledder are limited.

Our body and our circumstances make up the physical, or what we term the "body." We can train this to a very high degree indeed. And if we have the right environment, we can excel as well.

One person may be an excellent pianist, but not have had the opportunity to perform. Another person may get what we call a "lucky break" and the skills are only developed to a certain capacity. Mozart was born with talent, a father who trained and honed in on that talent, and at a time that appreciated his talent. We often blame one or another of our "body" components for not attempting something new. For example, "I can't play a musical instrument, I'm too old," is a common one I hear. The environment may not be right for a person to learn an instrument and be famous in learning to play the piano, for example, but they can always learn. The joy is in the learning. It holds true for all that we can learn or attempt.

Of course, there are certain disabilities that may hinder someone from moving into any one thing. Someone who is visually impaired may not appreciate a painting the same way as someone who can see. However, they can still participate in the act of painting, the touch, and the kinesthetic aspects. Again, in the world of running, when I'm at the track and run with people who have lost a leg, I'm inspired that the "body" of our lives may challenge us, but is never the reason not to attempt something new in this life. It is the *earth* of us that has the universe work through us.

As we are the only one of us to walk on this planet—and this universe—what we bring to every situation is unique and should be attempted. Whether we find fame and fortune is irrelevant. If we experience joy and facilitate learning, then we are in the right place. The process warrants the attempt. The body is the vehicle we use. Granted, this vehicle is sometimes a broken-down jalopy, but at other times it is a sleek Maserati. In our lives we work to craft and shape our body.

MIND: the learning we acquire. We improve, get better, or just try something different. This may be in any endeavor. The need to improve and learn is inherent in humans. From an early age, we crave to improve; it starts with crawling and walking and speaking. When we are in school, many new students are eager to learn new subjects. Whether the teachers meet that eagerness is a different matter. I see the same when hiring new employees—they are eager to do an excellent job, learn the elements of the job, master them, and be successful.

Sometimes it's a hobby, craft, art, or sport that drives a person to improve. Someone wants to learn a certain stitch for a quilt, another to build a ham radio, and for some to find that numismatic rarity. Some insistently practice their golf swing thousands of times to lower their handicap. Others may practice scales over and over to master the ability to slide smoothly into the notes of a trombone.

The point of the matter is that this learning ability is continuous in us all; and sometimes, in some areas, we may have been frustrated or told that we are no good and give up. But in other areas, we may excel. We may have given up on the joy of math because our fourth grade teacher told us our multiplication skills were a bit sloppy. Or given up on music because playing scales on the piano when we were seven years old was just too boring for our active personality. Others may give up on sports because they hated gym class or because they only won a baby-shit green colored "Good Sportsmanship" ribbon.

What may have been true when you were seven years old may not be relevant to you now. Though the message may have come across strong and the belief in what was told hinders us from trying again, it doesn't prohibit us from going out and trying new things.

The mind craves learning and the constant progress of growth. The more you feed your mind, the greater your well-being. For some people, this may be learning very deeply about one subject. For another person, this may be learning about several subjects all at once. Whichever pattern you chose, the point is to learn. The mind craves it; the spirit craves it.

SPIRIT: the energy, joy, and enthusiasm we have. This word may get people into a religious frame of mind; however, I ask you to resist that temptation. I like the word "play" better, as it conjures up the images of childhood. When children play, they forget the world around them; they focus on one thing, lost to the outside world. Watch a child playing on the beach. She will use her imagination to build up hills, create towns and walls, using sticks for different people, speaking in different voices to herself.

There is abandonment of the social norms of success or practicality. It is just life and living. The body and mind are completely engaged in play—in the spirit. The same happens when kids play a sport or a game and there is concentration and abandonment.

When you look in the dictionary at all the ways that we use the word "play" you can feel the energy of the human spirit for games, sports, music, performance, sex, movement, and pretending.

This spirit that charges our world is what we tap into to bring enthusiasm to an activity. The word *spirit* comes from the Latin, meaning "to breathe." This spirit, breath, is something everyone can tap into. Some may have a religious connotation wrapped around it, which is fine, but it is bigger than that and more open than the confinement of religious dogma. It is a force that moves through us that any of us can tap into to live our lives more fully, creatively, and openly. It engages us in our mind and body so that all three can synchronize to work together.

#SWEET SUCCESS: For this exercise, set aside one hour. For ten minutes, write non-stop, without much thought, what *body* means to you. In the next ten minutes, write about *mind*. And last, for ten minutes, write about *spirit*. In each of the writings, pour out everything. Again, no editing. This is just a free flow to explore your thoughts and thinking.

Then for the next twenty minutes, go through and underline and highlight any words that stand out to you or any thoughts that resonate with your understanding. Last, jot down any insights that you have from the exercise about your own thinking of body, mind, and spirit.

#AGE 10

Let's go excavating your memory again. We can remember what we did, but there are blanks, and some of those blanks we fill in. The parts that we remember are sometimes very distinct, be it a smell, song, image, or person. Around these your memory, a creative wonder, starts to add in details that you thought you forgot.

Let's use that wonderful memory to take a look at who you have been in your life. Certain aspects of your personality persist throughout your life and stay with you. Many aspects of your ten-year-old self will still be apparent to you today. When you were ten, much of the world still felt new and fresh. Your parents, relatives, and friends would all have a strong impact on you. The places you visited, such as your school, parks, and vacations would also have formed your experiences that helped make up a bit of who you are today.

Another challenge is that we sometimes have traumatic, sad, or horrible experiences when young. Going back and looking at these experiences as well, exploring your feelings and memories around those times, helps you better respond to them now that you're older. Often times, traumatic childhood events are carried with much more weight and regret and emotion. They are given too much space in our adult lives. To face these events head-on, explore how they have molded and shaped you as a person. Give credence to the event, but in a way such that you control the memory, not that the memory controls you.

His uncle had sexually abused Kenneth when he was five years old. The event had created anger for him and a strong distrust of people. He especially felt uncomfortable with intimate, male relationships, and harbored much anger. When he went to explore his childhood, he found the memory was not so terrifying as he had made it, acknowledged the anger, and was able to move on from it.

In contrast, sometimes an event may be wonderful and fills you with ecstasy of that happy memory so that you have not moved on. This is being trapped in the "good ol' days" and realizing that they were filled with joy. But if we remain stuck there, we threaten the happiness that can be found in the present.

Sam, at ten, was excellent in sports. He excelled everyone in tennis and by high school was the captain of the tennis team and class president. He had exceptional good looks as well. He entered university on a scholarship, but an injury kept him from progressing any further in tennis. He graduated, got a job, and married his high school sweetheart. Everything in life came easy to him. Then he lost his job, blaming the system. Lost his health insurance, and again the system was to blame. His drinking and overeating were taking a toll on his health, but there wasn't any problem. Then a driving while drunk charge put him in jail. His wife left him. It wasn't until Sam could see that he was in control of the decisions he was making that he understood what he needed to do.

We find ourselves trapped in good or bad memories. The ability to explore them objectively will build your emotional maturity. Exploring the childhood things that happened, those with wonder and joy or those with sadness will help you discover the person you are today. As Socrates said, "An unexamined life is not worth living." Investigating your life and knowing who you are provides you with rich experience and meaning.

#SWEET SUCCESS: In your CB, take twenty minutes and write. What would you tell your ten-year-old self to do to make a better now? We often live in the past and make excuses because of it: poor education, not enough money, abusive parent, wrong place, time, and culture—whatever. Well, get over it. Have your ten-year-old self tell you what you need to do now and forget about the past; live in the present.

#WHEN I'M 64

"Will you still need me, will you still feed me when I'm sixty-four?"

—The Beatles

Wisdom can often move us in the right direction. And often, with age comes wisdom. I know that as I age, I have learned to be patient, empathetic, sympathetic, inquisitive like a child, and accepting like a friend, as well as forgetful, forgetting the glasses on my forehead, and going to the bathroom five times a night. When I go back and read journals of what I wish I could do better or what I would tell my older self to do, these traits are definitely ones I lacked, but gained with age.

As you project yourself forward in years, you'll ask yourself questions about how you should act and what you would like to do. Your older self may be a bit more relaxed, carefree, and wise than you imagine.

In many cultures, it is the old people of the tribe and clan who are listened to. In Homer, Nestor, the oldest member of the Greek army, was often asked for his council. We give special place to the wise and you can do that from your own wisdom of yourself.

#SWEET SUCCESS: Take out your commonplace and write for twenty minutes without stopping. Imagine you're on your deathbed. You have your loved ones gathered around. You also have your present-day self there. What have you accomplished in life? What would you tell a younger you?

#SWEET SUCCESS: From your writing at age 10 or age 83, take one item and put it into action. As mentioned previously, who you are to be you are now being. Why wait until you're 83? Start being that person now.

#TIME FLIES

Many people are enslaved by time. They go about their day glancing at their watch or smartphone, each moment measured out "with coffee spoons" (T.S. Eliot). I know that I'm guilty of living by the clock, the calendar, and the to do list. Of course, we reward such a habit. The point is to remember that it is indeed a habit. When you started out, as you might remember from other previous writings in your CB, childhood was timeless. You could only conceive of morning, play time, bath time, which was a bad time, and bedtime, which was another unpleasant event. Next, the year started to be measured out by birthdays and Christmas, and if they were lucky enough to fall on the same day, then there was only one special day a year until school started. And then the seasons came and the start of school and winter break and spring and summer break and the start of a new year. Eventually, someone taught you how to read a clock and then you found a watch stuck on your wrist. You were officially enslaved by time.

A bit of a side note—though watches had been around since the 15th century, it wasn't until the turn of the 20th century that wristwatches came into vogue. Women wore them as jewelry and men sported pocket watches. With the dawn of war comes progress, and the same held true for the watch, which found its way onto men's wrists in the trenches of World War I. However, it wasn't until the 1960s and the invention of quartz watches when the wristwatch became a normal, everyday item.

Now back to our regularly scheduled program.

So here you are, sitting barefoot, staring at the pages of this book or at an electronic version, and you have a watch on your wrist and probably didn't even think much about it. It was just a simple thing that happened somewhere between high school and starting to work. Probably about the time you lost your virginity and needed to remember when you needed to meet your date.

It's an interesting experience to remove your watch for a couple of weeks. You'll not only gain a bit of freedom, you'll also gain insights on where all the other clocks and watches are in the world. You will learn to look at other people's wrists during lunch to see how much time you have before the next meeting. You'll cock your head at a strange angle to read the watch on the woman's wrist sitting across the room and she'll slightly move away from you. You'll see that the bank at the intersection you cross every morning actually has a clock and you never noticed. If you want to take it to another level, hide away your smartphone for periods of the day and see how you cope.

The idea here is to open up your awareness. First, to the habit you have. Second, to realize that time is your most precious commodity. By not measuring it all the time, you'll actually participate and cherish it more. You'll also free up some arm space if you would like to wear that turquoise bangle or silver Tiffany bracelet.

#SWEET SUCCESS: Rid yourself of your watch for two weeks. Try to live in the world without time—or at least a little less meticulous measurement of it. Learn how many ways you can find out the time. Shake yourself out of your normal world and take off your watch. As the great physicist Erwin Schrödinger wrote, "For eternally and always, there is only one now, one and the same now; the present is the one thing that has no end." And thank your lucky stars that you're not Schrödinger's cat!

Each day in your CB, record your reactions, observations, and frustrations. And realize that you may find yourself late when you were never late before or early when you used to find yourself late. Time, as well as your life, will start to shift.

#LET THEM EAT CAKE

Hippocrates, the Father of Medicine, born in 460 BC and lived to a ripe old age of ninety, said, "Let food be thy medicine and medicine be thy food." In the study of body, mind, and sprit, food needs to take a front row seat. We all eat, every one of us, so we all have opinions about what makes for a good meal. For some it will be taste, some presentation, others comfort, and still for others food will carry a religious significance. Hippocrates' quote resonates with the modern computer principle, GIGO—Garbage In, Garbage Out. If you eat crap, then you will feel like crap; or to be more positive, if you eat well, you'll feel better.

As Roberta Anding reports, a trend study from the American Dietetic Association suggests that 43 percent of Americans believe that they are eating well, and yet the United States Department of Agriculture has shown that Americans have increased their daily food intake by 523 calories since 1970. If nothing else, the amount of food we eat—the serving size—has greatly increased. Let's face it, in the 1970s there were much fewer 4XL sizes or venti lattes or Super Big Gulps. A Super Big Gulp of cola has about 35 teaspoons of sugar. So probably, serving sizes have played a part in changing Americans' body proportions.

In eating well, there are some simple guidelines that are much easier than all the fad diets. In my humble opinion, if you do these five things, you can start to eat better:

- Eat moderate portions.

- Eat vegetables and fruit.

- Minimize sugars.

- Stay away from processed food.

- Abstain totally from soda, including diet soda.

Remember, for the *body* of you, a good diet determines how you act and feel. Any athlete will tell you that their performance will often be determined by the food they eat. Many vegetarians will tell you that meat-eaters smell differently. Take all this to heart. Don't worry about cutting anything out of your diet, but work on placing good things in your diet to force out the bad.

As a marathon runner who logs a lot of time out running, I've found that the importance of good nutrition magnifies itself. If I binge on chips and ice cream, and I love chips and ice cream, I feel it in my performance. When I fuel for a run, I find that oatmeal works better than a slice of bread with peanut butter and way better than a bowl of fruit. Pizza doesn't work; a banana does. I admit it though—a good pizza is a beautiful thing! Find a balance. Rather than a pizza every day, go for that thing of beauty once a month.

I'm not advocating any sort of diet or weight loss program. Most of them seem to me to be fads or quick ways to make money. I really don't like drugs as a way to lose weight. Again, I subscribe to Hippocrates' idea above. What I am saying is that if you want to live a long life and have sweet ideas throughout your life, then you should eat more natural foods and abstain from processed ones; it's that simple. Personally, I think McDonalds and Coca-Cola have done more to destroy people's health in the U.S. and other parts of the world than almost anything else. In Japan, my home for the last 20 years, I've witnessed firsthand how the fast food market has developed and literally changed the shape of people's bodies.

With the negative, though, there is much positive as well. I think Jamie Oliver is a superhero. He has done so well to teach people how to cook easily and quickly. His recipes are varied, taste good, and are healthy. The Internet as well has great healthy recipes. And the ability to find inexpensive ingredients has spread over the years.

#SWEET SUCCESS: Keep this simple. Rather than cutting out food, start adding food. What one food can you add to your diet that would help you? In our office, afternoon snacks of chips and sandwiches were replaced with tuna in water and avocado or tomatoes—a simple, quick, healthy snack. Maybe you'll want to add a glass of soy milk each day. Or perhaps replace chips with almonds. Or once a week, instead of ice cream, have cut fruit or yogurt. Whatever it is, find something that you'll love to eat and that is good for you. And then eat it. The work on your nutrition will help you enjoy more meals, remain healthy, and stay fit for a long life.

#READING

I know I'm preaching to the choir. After all, you're reading this book. But I'm going to challenge you in this section and in several other sections about your reading habits. Of course, there are many other valuable ways to learn, especially in this wonderfully content-rich era. I'll try not to sound like an old fuddy-duddy, telling you to read old, dead, white European men, though I have to admit there are worse places to start. Some of those dead, white European men knew their shit. And let's face it, some of it was boring rubbish. So let's try to steer our way clear to see some of the good, bad, ugly, and also some of the fun. If you're only reading one sort of book, you'll be dull, and that isn't good.

So what to read? My first answer would be everything and all things that appeal to you for a start. I met my friend Craig for lunch and he told me that he had stopped reading fiction as it was taking away from his "serious reading." I was shocked, as some of the best learning and insight I've ever had was from fiction. As another friend told me, he was reading Mario Puzo's *The Godfather* while reading about management, and the cross pollination was insightful, with examples and consequences much further reaching than what could be found in only a management textbook. There are no severed horse heads in *The One Minute Manager*, *First Break All the Rules*, *The Effective Executive*, *The 7 Habits of Highly Effective People*, or *The Essential Drucker*. Where better than fiction can you see these ideas played out and challenged? Granted, I feel that Shakespeare, Goethe, Mark Twain, and Virginia Woolf have more to teach than Tom Clancy, Stephen King, and Danielle Steel, but that doesn't mean that the latter are without merit. For me, as I've written elsewhere, Agatha Christie has been one of the best teachers of sales, along with Dr. Seuss's Sam-I-Am, who asks good questions, listens, and persists; that's *Sweet Sales* in a nutshell.

History too, expands our insights into what has flowed before us and encompasses all of the other fields. And specifically from history, biographies of individuals can show you the possibilities of the human condition. See how Alexander the Great conquers the known world; sail with Magellan through the seas; tap into the creation of a new music with Duke Ellington. We can learn how governments act and individuals react, and see how history relates to families and work politics as well.

Poetry, which also gets a whole section, also holds an exceptional place. A poem's images, rhythms, and turns of phrase can describe the indescribable with such unbelievable emotion. To bring the life and experience of the world into a few short lines is amazing. Some teachers make poetry hard. Of course, learning techniques and marking out measures and finding symbols and metaphors can deepen meaning, but they can also be a barrier to just starting out and learning the liquidity and music of words and the joy and insight of the juxtaposition of two seemingly different images.

In 7th grade, on our reading day or a day we did homework in class, Mr. Bowman would play The Moody Blues' "Nights in White Satin" or Led Zeppelin's "Stairway to Heaven" and tell us that that was poetry. Poetry was alive, everyday, and real. He also made us memorize poems and stand in front of the class and recite. The poetry has stayed with me over the years and still gives me solace. Though I can't recite it word for word anymore, many of the turns of phrase and images live with me. Let me share with you some of the lines that have stayed with me:

Shakespeare's "Sonnet 2"

When forty winters shall besiege thy brow
And dig deep trenches in thy beauty's field,
Thy youth's proud livery, so gazed on now,
Will be a tattered weed, of small worth held.
Then being asked where all thy beauty lies—
Where all the treasure of thy lusty days—
To say within thine own deep-sunken eyes
Were an all-eating shame and thriftless praise.
How much more praise deserved thy beauty's use
If thou couldst answer "This fair child of mine
Shall sum my count and make my old excuse,"
Proving his beauty by succession thine.
This were to be new made when thou art old,
And see thy blood warm when thou feel'st it cold.

This taught me the importance of carrying on the beauty that I had when I was in 7th grade. Now my sons "sum my count and make my old excuse" and it does warm my blood.

Shakespeare's Sonnet 29 taught me the importance of keeping friends.

When in disgrace with fortune and men's eyes,
I all alone beweep my outcast state,

And trouble deaf heaven with my bootless cries,
And look upon myself and curse my fate,
wishing me like to one more rich in hope,
Featured like him, like him with friends possessed,
Desiring this man's art, and that man's scope,
With what I most enjoy contented least;
Yet in these thoughts myself almost despising,
Haply I think on thee—and then my state,
Like to the lark at break of day arising
From sullen earth sings hymns at heaven's gate;
For thy sweet love remembered such wealth brings,
That then I scorn to change my state with kings.

We had to memorize the first stanza of T.S. Eliot's "The Love Song of J. Alfred Prufrock." These lines still haunt and delight me in sound and image. Often, when speaking to someone, I'll say to her, "Let us go then…" and the rest of the image warms my being.

Let us go then, you and I,
When the evening is spread out against the sky
Like a patient etherized upon a table

I love it so much, I put it at the beginning of this book.

And I remember struggling with the long William Butler Yeats poem, "The Second Coming." But to read these words out loud, even without grasping the meaning, the music created is exceptional.

Turning and turning in the widening gyre
The falcon cannot hear the falconer;
Things fall apart; the centre cannot hold;
Mere anarchy is loosed upon the world

And what sex-crazed, horny 7th grade boy wouldn't love Yeats' "Leda and the Swan"?

How can those terrified vague fingers push
The feathered glory from her loosening thighs?

Then there was Archibald MacLeish, who wrote the coolest turn of phrase that a 7th grader would hear:

Quite unexpectedly as Vasserot
The armless ambidextrian was lighting
A match between his great and second toe

What the hell was an "armless ambidextrian"? Oh, that was fantastic! The whole image quite unexpectedly blew the top off my mind.

Poetry is alive and it shows us the potential of our world. Slip off your shoes, have a sandwich of sprouts and avocado, and read a poem.

And let's not forget the sciences. If I was stuck on a desert island, the one book I'd take with me is Euclid's *Elements*. And if I could take two, I'd ask for the Greek version of Euclid and a Greek dictionary. His proofs were as beautiful as Bach's Partitas. Of course, it took time and a great teacher to help me understand geometry and move past what I had learned in public school. In junior high, when I first met geometry, I felt frustrated and Dad helped me with the proofs and understanding the theorems, but to no avail. In graduate school, a great teacher, Teri Martin, showed me the historical significance and it became much more interesting: to realize that Euclid was simply trying to describe the ideals of the known world in shapes—trying to mentally describe perfection. The idea influenced me so much that I based my doctoral studies on Buckminster Fuller's geometrical ideas of synchronicity.

Philosophy and religion give insights into the human condition as well. Open up to the human condition, suspend closure, and allow your mind to open. Enjoy the Greek and Roman myths. The epics of Gilgamesh, Homer, and Moses. Learn to ask hard questions like Socrates and Nietzsche, and then spend some time thinking about the answers. They will lead to more questions and more answers until you're forced to suspend closure even more.

Nearly every room in my house had a library, but my Dad's den was the most classic. The room had a wood floor covered by my great-grandmother's oriental carpet. My Dad had built a shelf for his books that filled the whole wall. I sat on the carpet and the books called down to me like a siren, and I would open them and smell the pages and read a few lines of Pearl Buck, Voltaire, or Robert Penn Warren's *All the King's Men*. My parents had a library and I was so lucky to have a set of *Compton's Encyclopedia* to thumb through. And there was a wall of books—John Steinbeck's *Tales of King Arthur*, and I felt scared going through all of Stephen King's horror. I remember the ones close to the floor, as I was short. I had to stretch to reach the eleven volumes of Durant's *Story of Civilization* or the complete works of James Fennimore Cooper. Sometimes I would stand on a chair and I could reach grandma's copy of Shakespeare from high school with an embroidered leather cover. And an antique copy of Mark Twain's short stories where I read the funny diaries of Adam and Eve. I say antique, but in this case, it was just an old book probably bought at a second-hand store. There was a college anthology of poetry I'd thumb through. And I loved to look at the mammoth atlas of the world.

I find that today, we have so much more access to books. On my tablet, nearly every classic is available in the public domain, so philosophy, history, and great stories are open to me for free from websites like the Poetry Foundation or Project Gutenberg.

Let me not forget to mention a bit about all the work that is also published online, such as blogs and websites. Blogs and websites contain a wealth of information that, like the library in Alexandria, it could be easy to get lost in. Dive in and look around and search for hidden gems and treasures. The wonder of these is that you can build a community that has far reaching and diverse ideas. Websites like Medium.com open up a world of writing on any subject one longs to read.

Try to read a new book often, maybe even one a month. And then jump into something different. If you usually read non-fiction, try a fiction book. If you read fiction, try non-fiction. If you read mysteries, try a classic, a Western, a fantasy, try history, try a book on math, read science, try a subject that you used to love in school but have since forgotten about. I used to love math in 7th grade, but then after a couple of bad experiences I fell away from math. Then in college, where I had an excellent teacher who taught me the sublime joys of Euclid, I returned to it and loved it.

Read outside your comfort zone and try something new. Steve Chandler wrote in his *100 Ways to Motivate Yourself* that smart people read murder mysteries. I thought to myself, "I'm smart!" But I did not read murder mysteries. I went out to the bookstore and bought three Agatha Christie novels and loved them!

Lastly, if you don't have a library card, get one! The wealth that is being unused and untapped at the library is amazing. There is no reason not to fill your mind with bright ideas every day of your life and all of it for free!

If you don't know where to start, look for something fun that you thought would be great to read. I'd also recommend *How to Read a Book* by Mortimer Adler. At the end of the book, there is a list of books that have changed the world, which is worth taking on as a challenge.

#COOKING

Cooking is an excellent way to have your creative juices start to flow. There is something relaxing, humbling, and artistic about chopping, cutting, dicing, and then serving it up, especially if you can serve it to someone else without slicing off a finger. Though I don't consider myself a chef of any merit, when I do cook I find the whole process very much like playing chemistry where I'm fixing the flavor of Food A with Food B and coming up with Plate C. What could be a better example of synergy where one plus one equals three? And leaving my finger attached is an added bonus.

Time in the kitchen, focused on accomplishing a task, is akin to working in a garden, building a deck, or fixing an engine motor. You're doing something kinesthetic and moving, mixing pieces and putting them together in creative ways. And even following a recipe provides you the freedom to pay attention to each action in a Zen-like way.

Take a meal and make it from scratch. Maybe an omelet—my favorite simple meal. I can basically grab a couple of eggs and then dice whatever I find in the fridge, be it some mushrooms, onions, lunch meat, peppers, or a bit of cheese.

You may also find something delicious on a website to challenge yourself. Find something that interests you—marinated chicken, a soufflé, enchiladas, coleslaw, muffins, or a Black Forest

#COOKING

cake. A friend of mine, who loves curry, went out and bought a book of curry making and then had an office curry night every few months to help inspire him. Make it as easy or as difficult as you'd like. If it tastes bad, just throw it out and learn from your mistakes. I added too much garlic to some hummus once and it would have scared off the most frightening of vampires. After many years of cooking, I had a new-found respect for spices in general and garlic specifically. My cooking has taken a turn for the better! I'm sure yours will too!

#SWEET SUCCESS: Cook a "new" meal this week. And preferably for someone, without slicing off your finger.

#MEDITATING

Dr. Britta Holzel, well-known researcher in the field of psychology and mindfulness, performed a study of people who mediated. She found that in the test subjects, the gray matter of their brain produced more neurons, which they retained over time (Yi-Yuan Tang, *The Neuroscience of Mindfulness Meditation*). In short, they got smarter.

For many people, the world moves very fast. Meditating is a way to slow down the world and focus your mind. With a few moments of concentration on your breath or just concentrating on concentrating, you can release your mind from the email, texts, social media, and all the other data that overwhelms the senses. Maybe even forget the noisy neighbor.

I was lucky enough that my mom taught me to mediate when I was around five years old. I was her noisy neighbor. Like most five-year-olds, I was rambunctious and hyperactive, moving and talking all the time. Just learning to count my breaths or to listen for ten minutes to Pachelbel's *Canon* relaxed and quieted me.

The other reason is that my mother had had several back surgeries and lived in pain. She used a form of meditation—biofeedback—to help control the pain. If you live with pain, physically or emotionally, a few minutes of restful mindfulness helps dull the sharp edges of that pain. By visualizing the areas that are in pain, breathing in warm, healing light, breathing out the hurt and sickness, you can increase the speed of the healing.

As I grew older and got more into marathon running, I found that many sports figures use visualization as a way to enhance their performance. Most Olympic athletes use some sort of visualization to improve performance.

The benefits are numerous and scientifically backed by many studies. One is that you will start to find the ability to quiet your mind, which allows you to make quicker and better decisions. You'll be less likely to be swayed by anger or other negative emotions. Of course, they don't disappear from life, but the ability to practice mindfulness helps you in being mindful and keeps them in check.

There are countless ways to meditate and I've found some good visual image-training guides on YouTube. However, here are two simple methods.

First, concentrate on your breathing. Watch in your mind's eye your breath going in and then watch as you exhale. You may have other thoughts that try to seep in while you do this. Acknowledge those thoughts and turn your attention back to your breathing. Simply concentrate on your breathing.

The second method is to concentrate on clearing your mind. Work to clear your mind of any thoughts. Take a couple of deep breaths, fully filling and emptying your lungs, and then work to clear your mind. Thoughts may come in and out. Let them float by and then try to usher them out.

Sit quietly, by yourself, even just for five minutes (to start with) and then listen and look. Quiet your brain and start to listen. The psychobabble, that constant talking we do in our heads, very often says nothing of importance. Imagine if you, like Einstein, could go fifty-six hours without listening to that voice in your head. You can, though it takes practice.

#SWEET SUCCESS: For one week, set three times to meditate for five minutes. Aim to do this for a month—that is, twelve five-minute sessions where you sit and quiet your mind. Even in the busiest of schedules, you can sneak away for five minutes and sit quietly with your own thoughts. Record your experiences in your CB. After a month, go back and reread your experiences and see if you've had any changes or insights.

#TEACHERS

When I started 7th grade, I met Mr. Craig Bowman. He loved to tell us of his childhood as an orphan raised by Catholic nuns who gave him an appreciation for classical learning, an old-time respect for others, a belief in living your potential, a love of the Catholic faith, and a foundation of the teacher as servant. He lived like a monk and probably would have been a good priest if he had ignored his calling to be an excellent teacher. His living room had two desks for writing, facing each wall. Above one desk was a painting of Thomas More. Above the opposite desk was Erasmus. These represented his heroes and encapsulated his philosophy of the Christian humanist. Not only did he teach us to write, he practiced writing himself and wrote a weekly column for the Rocky Mountain News. He also played organ and I was lucky enough to sit next to him when he went down to the Air Force Academy in Colorado Springs and played Bach. He was also kind enough to play at my wedding. When he played, his whole body swayed and he was enraptured with the music.

In the classroom, he made middle-class suburban kids stand when an adult entered. We had to diagram sentences and memorize lists of prepositions. As mentioned, we stood in front of the classroom and recited from memory Shakespeare, T.S. Eliot, Abraham Lincoln's "Gettysburg Address," and even selections from the King James Bible. Though the public school would never agree to teaching the Bible, Mr. Bowman sneered at this because the King James was some of the greatest English literature, regardless of anyone's religious beliefs—good writing trumped dogma.

In 7th grade, twelve years old, he gave me a research paper to write on, "The Territorial Imperative in Human Beings." WTF?! I had no idea what that phrase meant when I started.

Occasionally, Mr. Bowman would walk into the class and ask us our opinions on abortion, teenage suicide, and the education system. We had to defend our ideas with reasons, not emotion, and we learned that our opinions backed with reason were important and valid regardless of their stance.

We learned that a 95 percent was an "A"—not 90 percent, like other classes. And if we were one point away from that higher score, even if we were a favorite student and a student helper, we still would be given the lower score—we had to earn our grade, as he prized excellence.

We laughed in Mr. Bowman's classroom when we learned that Shakespeare had plenty of dirty references to coitus and codpieces like in *The Merchant of Venice* when Gratiano says he will "mar the young clerk's pen." This joke spread into laughter and we were quipping, "My pen exploded in my pocket," and "My pen is long and hard and filled with ink." We enjoyed Chaucer's "The Wife of Bath's Tale" and learning in Boccaccio the meaning of making the "two backed beast." What thirteen-year-old boy would not be impressed with literature?

We had to memorize the opening of *The Canterbury Tales* in Middle English and, yes, recite it in front of the class.

On the first day of class, Mr. Bowman wrote his home phone number on the board and encouraged us to call him if we needed to talk. Not only me, but also several students used his phone number over the years if there were problems or challenges. We had three suicides in our school that year, but as a teacher as servant, he was there for us and told us, "He loved us."

He hated affirmative action and told us that too. He wanted to be judged based on his merit as a "teacher as servant" and writer, not on the color of his skin. He wrote beautifully to show us that we too could grow up and live up to our potential, despite our birth status, skin color, economic standing, creed, or any other PC excuse the government might provide.

Mr. Bowman related to us, but never stopped being a teacher. He loved the children and wanted us to learn and challenged us to grow. He believed that the teacher as servant served the children and parents and probably, for him, it also served God.

All this he taught, but also he was a model of the proper behavior, responsibility, and duty of an adult. When in junior high, and all the way to college and after, I would have lunch with him and we would speak about the merits of Shakespeare or the duties of teachers. He would meet with groups of kids on the weekends for lunch. There was something about his caring that kept us tethered to improving ourselves, learning, and being a part of the world. He was a teacher who guided, partly by his own art and writing and also as a role model. He taught poetry and writing and the importance they would hold later in life when going into sales, becoming doctors, medical supply representatives, interior designers, or recovering alcoholics. He showed the excellence and deep respect for quality that we should expect. He knew that our lives would have peaks and valleys and believed that literature and learning could help carry us through the highest joys and the darkest sadness. He lived what he taught—his actions and beliefs were always congruent.

Mr. Bowman was a humanist who embodied the importance of the human and shared that with his students and it became something that we could incorporate into our entire lives.

#SWEET SUCCESS: For fifteen minutes in your CB, jot down memories of your favorite teachers. Who were they? What did they look like? What made them your favorite? What did they teach you? Do you still use what they taught you?

#DREAMING

Since recorded time, humans have been guided by their dreams. King Menelaus, Abraham, Jacob, Xerxes, and Julius Caesar were all guided by their dreams. Sigmund Freud and Carl Jung brought dreams to the forefront of our world and gave us a subconscious paradigm to work from to describe these powerful images and impulses. André Breton brought dreams into modern art and some of my favorite artists—Max Ernst, Salvador Dali, and Jean Cocteau—created in that vein.

This morning, I had a dream and took out my CB and wrote down what I could remember. It was a strange one, but thankfully clean, or this would have been embarrassing. I was standing in a marketplace with shops on both sides. It was a bit like the fairground of a circus, but a bit more established with permanent buildings. People were walking into restaurants. And then the boxers arrived. Some people were like "Executive Fight Night" level of fighters. They were drinking beers and washing up and changing clothes. I remember two large men, powerful biceps, and bald. They came into the marketplace and there where stalls set up where they were bathed, shaved, massaged, and prepared for the boxing match. I wandered around this forum. People started thinning out to head inside the one restaurant that hosted the match. There were lights all around and it could have been in Las Vegas. I even saw a person I had worked with over 20 years ago. His name is David as well (though I can't remember his last name). He was in charge of safety and health at our company. I said, "Hello," and he went in to watch the boxing. I walked along and then the dream shifted into another place, just as dreams do. I walked onto an elevator that moved both vertically and horizontally, not just up and down, and it took me through an apartment complex. Because it was a low-rent apartment, the elevator went through everyone's living rooms and kitchens. The elevator at these intersections had guardrails blocking anyone from hopping on or off. The elevator sped up. I eventually ended up at a room where an old hippie lived. He was in his small room with only a bed and a couple of friends. He was not happy to see me because the person I had been with was rude. So he sent us away.

That is the entire dream I remember from this morning. Some parts of the dream may make sense to me, other parts are just images. But I find that when I write down my dreams, the images follow me throughout the day. Some of the images I may see. Or perhaps I saw them the previous day and my brain is categorizing them. There are scientific reasons for the brain to dream and this is why sleep is so important. But I also like to tap into the creative portion of dreams.

Creatively, dreams make you view the world from another point of view. Today, as I go about my routine, I'll think of that market square and think about bald boxers and Executive Fight Night. The echo from the dream will resonate and I'll look at things I generally take for granted in a new light, such as elevators. And was it a coincidence that there were bald men or someone named "David" in the dream? Sometimes there are connections, sometimes not. Our rational mind likes to make connections, so oftentimes we can find links.

This connection is what Carl Jung called synchronicity and is an excellent idea to explore. Synchronicity is bringing two seemingly unrelated events together into a meaningful coincidence. For example, when I'm talking to someone about a person who happens to call at the same instant. Or if I dream about a bald boxer and then see a poster for Executive Fight Night and there are bald boxers on the poster. Though not fully explored, Jung felt synchronicity was some of his most important work. I encourage you to look for synchronistic events in your life, and when they happen, pay attention and follow their lead.

#SWEET SUCCESS: This is a simple exercise. First thing when you wake up in the morning, write down any part of your dream that you remember from the night before. Set a timer for five minutes and write as quickly as you can. Then go back over what you wrote and see if any of the images resonate with you. Are they telling you anything? Are they asking you to take action? How do the images make you feel? What should you do differently today because of your dream last night?

If the answers fail to come naturally, don't force the answers. Just accept that a dream may be just a dream. As Freud said, "Sometimes a cigar is just a cigar."

If you find yourself really interested in dreams, set your alarm to wake you in the middle of the night and then write down your dreams. Your eyes may be a bit blurry when you write, but when you read what you wrote the next morning you'll better recall your dreams. Like any muscle, the more you exercise it, the stronger it becomes. As you pay more attention to dreams, your mind expects it and you'll recall them more easily each day. The insights will bridge your sleeping and waking self.

#GOALS #PROMISES #VISION

There is a lot written about goals. I hate goals. They strike me as limiting. You reach them and there is nothing more. Even as a marathon runner who has a goal of running a sub-three-hour marathon, there is something that just falls short. Once the goal is achieved, all is done. Goals also limit the ability of synchronicity, chance, and random opportunities that may present themselves but be overlooked.

I'm in a minority, I know. There was a Harvard study where students who wrote down their goals accomplished more in their lives than those who didn't. That might be the case, but to me it is more important to live a great life rather than simply accomplish a goal. Goals only look to the outcome rather than the process. For some, the outcome may be a long, long way. To start out on the venture, a focus on process is more beneficial. The sub-three-hour marathon may never be reached, but the joy of daily running and learning how to race faster is an awesome aspect of my life, which brings great happiness. Even if I never reach the goal, the daily improvement is outstanding.

The definition of a goal is "The object of a person's ambition or effort; an aim or desired result." There is something wanting here. It rests on a single person's effort driven by ego and cause-effect—you think of a goal, and it happens. Or it doesn't. Does it really matter? We may set big, hairy, audacious goals that drive us forward, and "though we may have not reached the stars, we did gather stardust." Phooey! This is saccharine, superficial, and a lot of fluff. Let's face it; if you reached for the stars and didn't reach them, you failed.

Also, goals lack emotion. They appeal to our logical side. We think of an ambitious executive who wants to climb the corporate ladder and she may have the goal to earn an MBA, to have a summer home, and travel first class to Bali. The goals tend to have materialistic aspects to them, nearly a wish. In contrast, if our ambitious executive focuses on process, she may find that to climb the corporate ladder she needs to improve, and it might be an MBA or maybe she could find joy in leading a charity or sitting on the board of a start-up company. In process, possibilities of other choices occur.

I prefer promises. A promise is an "assurance to someone that one will definitely do something or that something will happen." If we promise to do something, it happens.

Think of promising a child. In our culture of movies, we show adults speaking to children and when they use the word "promise" we know that everything in a person's power will be done to accomplish the act. For our inner child, we need to keep the promise. Our inner child wants to learn new things and open to the world, play, create, and learn. And not just for fastidious reasons, such as goals present, but to live a whole life. The inner child may have psychological aspects to it, but the fact is there are parts of our lives that seek to be new, fresh, reinvent, grow, driven to learn. We sometimes call that the beginners mind. This is what we need to cherish and protect, to grow in our lives. We need to build promises to that inner child and keep those promises. There is something emotionally charged around a promise.

Both goals and promises have the potential to drive us forward in our lives. But neither of them are much good without having vision to drive them. Visions are well known throughout history. We hear of dreams being followed as both promises and warnings. Sometimes they are described as a clear "flash" of intuition. Other times, they are a "soft voice" that drives consistent actions. These visions can drive us, warn us, or appear as an intuition. Like Saul who, when he heard the voice of God, followed that voice. I had a friend who smoked and he heard a voice that said, "Dammit, stop smoking!" Not the nicest of voices, but he followed it. For me, I sometimes hear a small whisper that guides me, and it may only be for small things, such as, "You're tired now, take a walk and think it over," or "Walk away and think about it," or "Go write that down."

Intuition may also be a source for us. An intuition is just that "feeling in the belly" or the "gut feeling" or just a tingling on the back of the neck. It's like a jockey on a horse, driving us on to take action. I've built companies that way and married based on intuition rather than facts and goals.

Vision, voices, intuition—I gather all under the vision: something that drives an individual on a higher plane. We may call this god or inspiration or muses or creative energy or the universe. The term isn't as important as the concept. We have the single point that drives us to take action. If we fail to take action on that vision, then we are acting against our true nature. This vision may go against our goals because vision is creative, often ambiguous, without language, and sometimes even without direction; we just "know" and then need to act. If we have closed off ourselves by only following goals, we limit ourselves to just facts and what our ego wants for us, severely limiting our ability to grow and reach new heights.

From your vision, you can take small actions that feel right. Set small promises and keep your promises. These kept promises gather momentum to build upon the vision and dreams of where you are going, with the ability to reach and surpass anything that a goal may have put down.

In my study of history, I find that goals tend to lead people toward horrible outcomes, whereas kept promises move the person forward with uncanny speed. Two examples from history. First, Napoleon, who, with the ideas and vision to unite the world, rid it of monarchy, and bring it a democratic peace, had a noble vision for the good of the people of Europe. The moment, however, he crowned himself emperor, he never again won another battle; he worked from goals and ego.

Another example is Captain James Cook, one of the greatest explorers ever. On his fantastic voyage on the *Endeavor*, he navigated and mapped for the first time the lands of New Zealand and Australia. He was true to his vision and, perhaps learning from a Quaker upbringing, open and amiable to his crew and the native peoples he met on his first two voyages. Then something happened on his third voyage, and though there is speculation that it could have been mental, I also guess that there were goals and ego behind his wanting to find the Northeast Passage, proving to the world he was the greatest. For the first time, he started being brutal to his crew and to the indigenous people he met, which ultimately led to his death in Hawaii (Sandwich Islands).

Undoubtedly, goals have the ability to move us forward. Promises, however, hold a strength and emotion on us, that move beyond simple steps. We seek higher powers to move us and accomplish them. There is something solemn and absolute in our uttering a promise, nearly a mystical quality. To grow, thrive, and challenge the world, listen to the small voices, follow your vision, move on intuition, and keep the promises of action.

#SWEET SUCCESS: Where do you find your vision? Where do you find your intuitive "aha" moments? That moment of epiphany? Take some time with your CB and write down a list of what you do when you have these insights. For me, I find it when I write each morning. I also find it when I'm on a long run—without any headphones. Also, when I draw pictures, do yoga, take walks through the city, sit in a library, shower, and drive. All these are alone. However, I also have "aha" moments when I sit with an executive coach (and often when I am the coach), when brainstorming ideas with the team, and a relaxed two or three people over a glass of merlot. How about you?

#NEXT RIGHT ANSWER

When you have an answer, look for the next right answer. This means that a person is able to suspend closure. They are not locked into regimented ways of thinking, dogmas, predictability, or mechanical thinking processes.

When interviewing people, the ability to suspend closure, to see more than one right answer, is a key element that I look for when hiring. It is easy to go into a situation with the answer already formed. The "right" answer is often one of many possibilities that can turn out to be wrong. Even when you have all the facts, you can still come up with the wrong answer.

For example, for the greater majority of human history, most people believed that the Earth was flat. If you traveled too far in any direction, you would fall off into an abyss. Even when some of the cumulative facts of over a thousand years were directly opposed, for the majority it was a safe, right answer. Even today, if you ask the average person on the street to prove the Earth is round, that person would be hard pressed to present the science that makes it true, and would rather pull up a NASA photo—a two-dimensional representation—of the Earth from space.

Facts are based on historical, past evidence and often become obsolete over time. Some things which five hundred years ago were astronomical facts are now dated, replaced by new facts based on better computers, telescopes, and critical observations of the charts and diagrams. In the future, maybe soon, many of these facts too will be proven wrong and our entire worldview will again change.

One of the ways to suspend closure and look for the truth is to play with your thoughts, look for more than one right answer. As Roger von Oech pointed out in his classic book *A Whack on the Side of the Head*, most people stop searching for answers after one has been found. Von Oech argues that, "This is unfortunate because often it's the second, or third, or tenth right answer which is what we need to solve a problem in an innovative way."

In our fast-moving world (hasn't every age found itself faster than the last?), we are expected to come up with quick responses and fast action. Email is the new "snail mail" and instant messaging in a variety of forms has taken the lead in communication. In fact, the ability to instantly answer in a variety of different mediums is expected.

However, to really thrive, have a creative life, and build a better world, we need to search for innovative answers. Not only finding one answer, but searching for five or ten answers. Then when you have a few answers you like, including ones you may not agree with, crazy ones, absolutely wrong ones, start looking at their opposites. Most bright ideas come from playing with what you "know." You must play and play well and seriously (not) play. When you have started the playing process, you'll generate more "right answers" and soon have more then you expected.

Please realize that finding more right answers is different from challenging already established answers. The process is not to tear away answers but rather to question and build. The starting premise is different. Someone who is challenging wants to point out how things are wrong. Sometimes this point of view is valuable, especially when it comes to safety issues and concerns. But when starting a new process and building out ideas, it's important to search for several possibilities and build from them a springboard.

The key takeaway is to be wary of facts and create more right answers. Go out and look up at the stars and look for the eternal truth. Do you see how that group of stars can guide the way, be it a bear, wagon, ox, dipper, plow, or a group of silent stars named Ursa Major? Maybe even a land where the great Flash Gordon would want to visit.

#SWEET SUCCESS: Take a problem you're facing at home or work and find twenty "right" answers. Keep your hand moving fast, don't overthink this, and set yourself a time limit. Twenty is a large number, which forces you to make some responses that may be silly, outlandish, contrary, and strange. Then take your challenge and look for the opposite and find ten more answers. Let's say you want to improve your work skills. You could sign up for a skills class, hire an executive coach, visit another office, read a book, etc. Then look at the opposite—how could you get worse at your job? Not show up, hire children, build a robot to take care of it, double the price, etc. Now if you start taking some of these ideas seriously and look at "not show up," in what ways is this relevant? Is it possible that parts of the position can be outsourced? Could you bring in an intern? What about building an application that would help you work from your mobile device? Play a bit and find the truth in the playing with the next right answer.

#INTENTION

Shutting down all the chatter of your mind and concentrating on where you're at in the moment is key to a more fulfilled life. With the disruption of modern-day mobile phones, SNS notifications on our watches, and a myriad of other items screaming for our attention, it's difficult to concentrate on the here and now.

The power of meditation, imaging, biofeedback, prayer, and all the other ways to quiet the mind is well documented throughout the world. The benefits associated with even as little as five minutes a day can lead to substantiated improvements in concentration and improved decision-making, as previously mentioned.

The other part is to have the intention to focus on the here and now. Often your mind will surge ahead and think about the day, worry about the meeting, how your team is performing, the Labrador and poodle walking down the street, your daughter's schoolwork, or needing to buy onions for the lasagna you'll make for dinner. Other times you'll think about the past, what was said, something that happened, a friend you miss. If your focus moves to the past or present, then intentionally move along with it. If you have the time, wallow in that moment and be present in the past or the present. There is much power in contemplating our past or dreaming about the future, but be present and do it with intent. If you are working now on a project, be there and put your energy into that project. Work with enthusiasm. Try to feel what you are doing, use your senses, and be aware.

I find that when looking at Instagram or YouTube, I can just fritter away the time and not even realize where my time has gone. The problem with this is that it causes our lives to pass by without our participation. Social media is designed to keep us engaged and enjoying their entertainment. When you are there, be there and enjoy them, but go with intent and focus and ask yourself—what are you really taking from the time spent there? Does it really enrich your life? You may know that Evel Knievel jumped 19 cars on a Harley (and if you don't know Evel Knievel, he is well worth the Google search), and he may seem important at the time, but it is now more trivial than important. To enjoy a sweet success sort of life, it's important to start taking stock of the trivial versus the important and live with intention toward the important.

It's challenging and only a few ever reach that enlightened spot where they live totally in the present and wander up onto a mountain in the Himalayas. Most of us have jobs and daily lives that tug us this way and that. By taking a few minutes to focus and then daily having the intention to move in the present, we can deeply engage in our life.

#SWEET SUCCESS: Are you still meditating? Good! I encourage you to continue!

Also, you may want to try Morning Pages. These were first presented by Julia Cameron in *The Artist Way* and have a huge following of supporters. In short, it is writing "three pages of longhand writing, strictly stream-of-consciousness." There is no wrong way to do it. Just get out a notebook, write three pages, then stop. This is not done on a computer. They need not be reread right away, and they are certainly not shown to anyone. If you don't know what to write, write about that for a bit. Repeat a word over and over. You'll get bored and then write something else. Doing this day after day centers you. It sometimes provides insights. Most of the time, they are dull.

In training for a marathon, there are a couple of days when I do very targeted training—speed work and long distance. The rest of the time, it is simply putting in the distance. Morning Pages are a lot like that. They allow you to chat, to observe, yell, vent, quip, recall, and ponder without any worry.

Try them for a month and see how your life changes. When you go back after a couple of weeks and read them, read them quickly and kindly without much expectation. You may find some bits of gold, but there will also be much rock around the veins. That is to be expected.

#CHOICES

Most of us are pretty good at putting a plan together. Come New Years, we scribble down a resolution or two or seventeen. Even if we don't write it down, we may have the plan mapped out in our mind. You decide this year you'll quit smoking or drinking, earn more money, you'll eat less Ben and Jerry's, watch less YouTube, read a book each month, or maybe not snack after 9:00 p.m. Perhaps you've decided to sign up for an online writing course, a CPA course, flamenco lessons, oil painting, Pilates, the local gym, or join a shogi club. Maybe it's to sign up for a certification so you can earn that promotion at work.

We usually know what we want to do and why we want to do it. On a diet, we don't want to eat ice cream, but more vegetables. But damn, ice cream is so good and cold and filled with the goodness of the universe that we eat an entire tub of Chunky Monkey. We should work out, walk during lunch. But then a friend at work brings a bag of Snickers for everyone to share, and they sit on the counter staring at you, until you take one…or two. Or maybe a project takes an extra hour and we decide to skip the gym. They are simple but understandable reasons. Yet, it was still a choice and the plan fell to pieces.

Then there is the series of choices we make all the time, saying "yes" to one thing and "no" to another. Personally, I wake up in the morning and write rather than do yoga. I go on a run afterwards instead of working on a current project. I eat breakfast rather than having a protein shake or skipping breakfast. I ride my bike to work instead of walking. I have water instead of coffee. I eat at the Japanese restaurant rather than the Indian one. All the choices weigh about the same. None of them are life shattering or derailing any plan or resolution. Our days are filled with hundreds of choices—the music you listen to, when to go to the bathroom, when to check email, to like or not like someone's post on Facebook. Some of the choices, like having a shower or riding a bike to work, are just set on autopilot and not thought about, making life run smoother, fitting a pattern so that I can accomplish more at work and life, such as writing, running, and sharing quality time with my family. Some of that day-to-day is predictable. And because it's automatic, I waste less time on it and get more out of a day. However, patterns can also bring about a dull routine, a rut, and finally stagnation.

That's why activities such as reading and travel are so important. They help you change parts, shift focus, and open your mind to other choices. Until I went to France, I never realized the importance of salt and butter in cooking and how special they could make my everyday food. Florida gave me a new appreciation for the ocean and seeing dolphins off the coast. Japan taught me to cherish personal safety. All these experiences dramatically shifted parts of my awareness, thinking, and the actions I took on a daily basis. In fact, in Japan I was shocked at how small the Ben and Jerry's ice cream cup was!

But let's face it, sometimes, on a daily basis, we make some "bad" decisions, like selecting a Snickers, just to mix up our lives a bit, spicing up our life with a bit of change. To reach more and do more with our lives, it's important to make good choices, ones that create patterns, and then to find constructive changes that open our lives to excitement, be it trying an exotic fruit, adding in a new exercise to our morning routine, or sitting in a different seat on the bus. As I said before, life is built upon the choices you make. Even when you decide not to choose, that's a choice.

The challenge is to strengthen the "choice muscle." Learn to choose quickly and often. The more you choose, the more selection you have in your life. Often you'll choose wrong. Often you'll choose right. When you go into a restaurant, there is rarely a life changing selection being offered. Look at the menu once then select quickly and assuredly. If asked by your spouse what you want for dinner, select something. When looking what to wear, quickly choose. Try not to hesitate.

This ability to choose will help you in executing those dreams and desires. Of course, you'll often regret a choice. But as the hockey Hall of Famer Wayne Gretzky said, "You miss 100 percent of the shots you don't take." If you want to succeed and execute your dreams, you need to choose. Life is built upon the choices we make.

#SWEET SUCCESS: Take out your commonplace and for fifteen minutes write about all the choices you make. Are there choices that are super simple for you to make? Are there choices that are difficult? What choices are you putting off? Why? What choices are others making that irritate you? Can you control those choices? What choices are you letting others make for you? What choices are you making for others?

- List five choices you have been putting off—make a choice.

- List five choices you can work to hesitate less on (for me, it was selecting off a menu at a restaurant).

- List five choices others are making. How can you take back the control of those choices?

Have fun with this exercise. Oftentimes, people who do this have the most profound understanding into what is happening with their life and find insights on how to take more control of their life and actions.

Choose what you want and plan in subtle changes to the choices on a regular basis to continue growing, learning, and keeping a bit of pizazz in your life within the vision you have set.

#EDUCATION

Many people blame their education for their status in life. They wish they had spent more time paying attention in algebra, studied more in physics, played a sport, kept up with the trumpet, put their drawing in the school show instead of feeling embarrassed. Some wish they had pursued their love of writing, others teaching, and some their passion for photography. Or maybe they finished school and successfully went on and earned a degree in marketing, but found out it was not for them, or entered law as their parents advised, but after a year of working in the profession, longed to teach. Some missed out altogether and know that if they had only had more classes or education, their life would be better. But whatever one's situation, it's good to remember that schooling is just school and from there we go on to careers. Sometimes the careers fit, and sometimes they don't. But a career, even if it doesn't meet our passion, can meet our life needs of raising a family, paying the bills, and providing for our life. There should be joy in that, which in turn can breathe new life into a career, family, and life in general.

It's not uncommon for people to feel that parts of their life have been missed. The real tragedy is that we abandon our dreams based on excuses rather than taking control of our lives and chasing new interests and dreams, even if they come to a dead end. We think that if we draw, we must be a da Vinci; or that to really learn the guitar, we should play like Ron Wood (sure, Keith Richards has more character and plays the riffs, but Ronnie is the better guitarist). In reality, the object of learning a new subject or skill comes in the learning itself. The outcome may have little relevance, though great importance.

You may have studied science and become a manager for a medical device company, but still have a longing to take photography. Why not sign up for an online course? At worst, you will learn new skills! However, the learning process will impact and change how you live your life in all aspects. As you learn a new skill, you may bring that skill into your medical device job, which impacts how you see the world.

Adam was a business owner stuck in his office day after day looking at Excel spreadsheets. Boring. Excel was a nice tool, but he thought those spreadsheets were as dull as watching snow melt. He would look at how to implement a new ERP system for the company and work with the finance manager and IT manager to get everything implemented correctly. He knew that part of the job was okay. However, he also had a real desire to paint. Not like Picasso or Cézanne, but like early Matisse. So on the weekends, he signed up for a painting class. "I was really terrible at the beginning," he said, "but just the mixing of paints was a real joy. Eventually, paintings emerged. Even my wife could tell what I had painted. What was really exceptional, though, was that I could see new ways to mix people at work like paints on a pallet. The creativity carried over into my work."

Mia was the head of Human Resources. However, what she really wanted to do was sell real estate. Though she felt it would take time, she started studying for her license. The following week after passing the exam for her realtor license, she got news at work that the office would be closing down. She wasn't worried, though, as this gave her a chance to start a new career. Now Mia is playing Monopoly for real.

Working in executive recruitment for over twenty years, I've seen many people who went through school, then jumped into a career. They felt a bit stuck, but didn't mind their job that much; it just wasn't their dream or passion. It lacked all the "umph" that Hollywood and all self-help books said you should have. The reality, in many of these cases, is that the person should concentrate on that career, then build a place in life to unplug—be it a hobby, a class, or simply some time alone. Just because we have fast-moving lives with Twitter and instant messaging and same day delivery doesn't mean we have to create careers that way. And education as well. Just because school stopped and graduation happened doesn't mean learning and education ends.

It's easy to think that our education was to blame or that we are stuck in a job. Accept your schooling. Work well in your career. And from time to time at lunch, slip your shoes off, dream, explore your desires, and take a small action into your dreams. Synchronicity follows and puts you on the path you need to go.

#SWEET SUCCESS: Here is your exercise. It's time for some creative thinking in your CB. Sit down and free-write for fifteen minutes about being born into the perfect education system—what would that system be? What would you study in elementary school, junior high, high school, and college and beyond? What would the curriculum be?

After fifteen minutes, stop. Go back and reread. Is there one thing that you can add to your life? What one thing can you give yourself to start working on your perfect education? Remember, no matter your age, you're never too old to learn something new. You may find an open class in your neighborhood or an online course. With the Internet today, there are so many options to find. Or maybe, you might find a friend or two and see if they would want to meet up once a month and together learn your new skill or craft. With a couple of friends, you'll have the support to move forward and learn.

Remember, education is part of a process, not an end point.

#DRESSING UP

Don't you hate it when you open up your closet or drawers and think, "I hate everything I own!" Nothing seems to look good. All your clothes are dull and you wonder how they got into your closet and drawers in the first place. Things may not fit—not just physically, but your mood. The materials clash with your skin, the patterns no longer inspire, the cut falls wrong across your body. "How come I have seven aloha shirts and a Joy Division t-shirt?"

There are days where you envy Steve Jobs, who probably felt this way once too often and had Japanese designer Issey Miyake make hundreds of the iconic black mock turtlenecks for him so he could refrain from having to think about what to wear. Like a uniform, he wore it over and over and didn't have to waste time thinking about what to wear. Definitely a stroke of genius, but for most of us, a bit dull stuck in a black turtleneck.

As Virginia Woolf wrote in *Orlando*:

Vain trifles as they seem, clothes have, they say, more important offices than merely to keep us warm. They change our view of the world and the world's view of us… There is much to support the view that it is clothes that wear us and not we them; we may make them take the mould of arm or breast, but they mould our hearts, our brains, our tongues to their liking.

When I was in elementary school, I used to find myself in the principal's office every other week. When I started middle school, my mom started using a bit of creative psychology on me. This was before public schools started requiring uniforms or students and teachers carried pistols to school. It was the "good ol' days."

"Let's do an experiment," Mom said. "For the next semester only, wear corduroys and sweaters instead of jeans and t-shirts. I bet your grades go up."

I figure you can guess the punch line. Of course, I raised my grades. Perhaps people looked differently at me or maybe I treated myself differently, but from then on I was able to avoid the principal's office and academically achieve more. Sure, I still did some things wrong, but regardless of it being right or not, because I looked like a good kid I started acting like one.

People do judge a book by its cover and they defiantly judge you by the clothes you wear. "But that's wrong," you may think. I agree, but it's still true. Many altruistic people may say they refrain from judging based on clothing, but having listened to hundreds of managers interview potential employees, I find that the opposite rings more true—everyone judges.

Our animal instincts let us know that someone may appear dangerous or safe based on how they are dressed. And let's face it, we like people who dress the part—police in uniform, a lawyer in a suit, a cook in an apron, and a doctor in a clean lab coat. Let's face it, a chef in a three-piece suit would not make a delicious soufflé and a doctor in a Boston Celtics jersey may make us a bit nervous.

#SWEET SUCCESS: Dress yourself differently for one week. If possible for your job, try to change one part of your wardrobe. If you wear suits every day, try polo shirts. If you wear wingtips, try Converse high-tops. If you are in a position that just won't allow this, then try it in your home life. If you wear jeans at home, try a dress; if you wear shorts, try slacks. One person told me that they could always tell rich people because they wore leather shoes when they traveled. Most Americans wear a form of athletic shoe when they travel. The Germans wear socks with sandals. Take the prejudices and try something new.

#MEMORY

If you can memorize ten items in an instant, you can wow your friends and neighbors. Of course, there are also some practical aspects to it. For thousands of years, some people were able to memorize vast quantities of information. Storytellers would travel from town to town, reciting epics, like Homer, with little variation between the telling. Messengers would have to memorize exact messages rather than writing things down. They had many methods for memorizing different items. And for me personally, my wife has been able to remember every single bad thing I've ever done.

I'll skip all the science and we can get right to the meat of the matter. First off, you have a perfect memory, but your recall is atrocious. So be it. To improve this, you need a system of being able to recall items in your memory. Being able to memorize helps train your brain, a bit like lifting weights helps to build muscles. The more you practice different recall methods, like the three outlined below, the easier it becomes. You gain confidence and feel capable of memorizing more things. Memorization also assists in visualization. By practicing to visualize, you activate creative parts of your brain, which is an added bonus.

You'll be able to use these techniques for simple items, such as a shopping list. Or you can memorize parts of a speech that you may have to give. The ability to speak without notes or PowerPoint will set you apart from other speakers and presenters, giving you an appearance of authority. You can prepare for exams, memorize the thirty most useful verbs in Japanese, all the countries in Africa, and the name of the ten major muscle groups of the body. The methods below are simple and fun to try. And if nothing else, being able to memorize ten items in an instant is a great party trick to amaze your friends over a martini.

Here are a couple of ways:

METHOD 1: For each number, make a rhyme with a word. Then really visualize the word. Picture the color, the sound, feel, movement of the object. Try to add all the senses—even taste and smell if you can. Make it crazy, fun, exciting, exaggerated, sexual (they say sex sells—well, in memorization sex often has strong emotive influences that, along with humor, make memorization easier).

Here are some suggestions; however, feel free to use your own, as your originals will make a longer lasting impression.

1: Sun

2: Shoe

3: Tree

4: Door

5: Hive (Bee)

6: Sticks

7: Heaven

8: Crate

9: Wine

10: Pen

For the number "one," I picture a bright yellow sun and can feel the warmth. It is radiant and has a face, just like I used to draw when I was a kid. It starts to sing, this happy sun, this number "one, sun."

Number "two," I think of my old marathon shoes. They may be a bit smelly to you, but for me there is nothing better than my pair of Adidas with the yellow stripe, with the white having faded a bit gray. Sometimes the pair of shoes starts to dance on their own! Two: shoes.

Now continue on through number ten. After you've done this, see if you can remember them. What was number one? Number two? And so on.

Now when someone says, "Memorize ten things," I link my picture with the object I need to memorize. For instance, if my wife wants me to buy some items at the store and I'm driving and can't write, I'll start imaging. She says, "Eggs, peanut butter, toilet paper, and gum." After each, in an instant, I'll start thinking, "One/sun = eggs." I'll picture throwing the sunny eggs at my picture of the sun. Splat! Splat! What fun! And then I'll think "Two/shoe = peanut butter." Imagine running the peanut butter marathon, slipping and sliding, thousands of New York marathoners running in peanut butter. Do this for each one, and you will remember, I guarantee it. All this only takes a second to memorize, as our minds work quickly to make images and links.

METHOD 2: Instead of rhymes, use the shape of the number to make a picture of the word to help you recall. Again, here are some examples, then go off on your own and find the shapes for the numbers and their objects that suit you best.

1: To me this looks like a straight Louisville Slugger "Bat"

2: The shape of the two, with the winding top, reminds me of the neck of a "Swan"

3: I imagine a three-pronged trident, like the water god Neptune carried

4: This looks to me like the puffed-out sail of a "Sail Boat"

5: A five-pointed star

6: A "yo-yo" with the string rolling down and then up again

7: A boomerang

8: An ice skating figure of an eight on a cold winter morning

9: A balloon on a string, circled part of the nine getting ready to float away

10: A straight arrow with a round target

The memorization technique is again the same. If I need to buy eggs, I picture myself doing some batting practice with them! Then for the peanut butter, I'll picture my swan, elegant on the river Thames eating a good ol' PBJ sandwich and then coughing it up, regurgitating for baby swans. I know, it's nauseating thinking of a swan coughing up bits of peanut butter, but you might remember it.

For this method as well, you can move beyond ten items. If you needed to remember item eleven, you think of two bats, and for twelve, a bat and a swan (bat being 1 and swan being 2, and so on).

METHOD 3: The *loci method* is at least 2,000 years old and was recorded by Cicero for the learning of rhetoric. It's a great way to remember several things for long term. It is a simple method of creating a place that you know well and having certain objects there that you can imagine. Some people may select a street, some a room, others a house. Sherlock Holmes had his "mind palace." I use my childhood house as I can remember much of it. We have a porch with a swing, in the door a closet, then the dining room to the left with a piano, a chair, a couch, and a dining table. Then to the kitchen, living room, bathroom, back yard. There is also an upstairs, attic, and basement. When I need to remember something, I place that thing in the place of my childhood house.

Again, taking our shopping list, I would think of big, Humpty Dumpty eggs on the swing of the porch, perhaps three or four swinging back and forth with big smiles. And then I walk into the door and in the front closet, I open it and all the coats are covered with peanut butter. For toilet paper, I may think of the piano in the living room. Perhaps the hammers of the piano are hitting on toilet paper rolls and making feces splatter across the room. Yes, I know it's repulsive to some, but hey, you'll definitely remember it.

The point to working on all three methods is 1) it's fun, 2) you work out your brain, and 3) you work out your imagination, especially the visualization. And to top it all off, you'll have an incredible memory and will be the life of the party. All of these advantages seem to me fairly good reasons for giving it a try.

#BIOGRAPHIES

Ahh, yes, even more on reading. In this section, we focus on biography. As William Boast and Benjamin Martin point out in *Masters of Change*, to excel in this fast-moving world you "start with the 'who to' rather than the 'how to.'" Biography helps you build a model of "who to" become.

Remember, the "how to" works for mechanical models. Mechanical models are closed systems that follow rules and steps. They are predictable.

In contrast, "who to" works for people. This model is organic, dynamic, and creative, looking at individuals as unique to this universe. When we use the term "who to," we have traditionally looked at a person's character. We think about the character of Elizabeth I, George Washington, or Winston Churchill and immediately a person comes to mind. These people worked throughout their lives on developing their character, and we can do the same. The quickest and easiest way is through modeling excellent character from biography.

Modeling isn't mimicking or searching for rules of a person's life. Modeling is watching the development of character, the response to challenge, the education and life choices that we see others have made. As we all have our own lives lived in our own context, there is no exact model—no "how to." In our own lives, if we have a challenge and think how a Steve Jobs or Margret Thatcher would handle the situation, creative responses from our own experience start to emerge.

From biographies, you can discover what happens to a young Albert Einstein who hates the rules of school but learns to live in the world of his imagination that he translated into physics. Observe a young Octavian as he develops from a scrawny lad to becoming Augustus Caesar, one of the greatest statesmen ever. Watch Teddy Roosevelt struggle from being a weak child into being a strength that the United States could lean on. Know, feel, and master within yourself the persistence of the Wright brothers and Thomas Edison. Feel the adventures of Capitan James Cook as he circumnavigates the Earth—more than once with a goat (having animals on board was not so strange, but for a goat to survive two circumnavigations of the Earth and return home to England is a fascinating story). Follow Catherine the Great as she tames and modernizes Russia. And for a rags-to-riches tale of character, read the life of John D. Rockefeller who became the richest man in the world.

When you dive into the biography of a great person, pay close attention to character. The reason you read biography is to develop your own. By looking at how others have lived their lives, what they have done and accomplished, the joys and tragedies of their lives, and even how they died, you start to build new thoughts and paradigms and truly understand what possibilities there are in this extraordinary life of yours.

The first biographer in history was Lucius Mestrius Plutarchus—or, thankfully, the much easier to remember *Plutarch* (AD 46–120), whose *Parallel Lives* was the first biography and compared the eminent Greeks and Romans. His work had significant impact on future generations, especially writers like Shakespeare, Boswell, and Emerson and leaders like Napoleon, Queen Elizabeth, and Teddy Roosevelt.

Born near Delphi in Greece, Plutarch was a Roman citizen who lived during the reigns of Claudius, Nero, and Hadrian and, even without the news of CNN, heard about the eruption of Mount Vesuvius burying Pompeii. He was born into a rich family, but ironically we don't know much about his biography. We do know he had a couple of brothers, married a woman named Timoxna, and had two sons and one daughter. He was educated in mathematics and philosophy at the academy in Athens and at some point became a Roman citizen. His life was prestigious enough in civic work and writing essays and histories that he was initiated into the mysteries of Apollo and was a trusted government civil servant.

Many of the stories in his *Parallel Lives* have made their way into popular fiction and movies. In his biographies, he starts with the mythic Theseus, the founder of Athens, and compares him to Romulus, the founder of Rome. He then moves to the lawgivers Solon and Numa, then historical figures so well known—Pericles, Alexander the Great, Julius Caesar, Pompey, Cicero, and Mark Antony. Some of the work has been lost through time, but his influence on all biography writers since is unrivaled. His biographies will inspire you and teach you to believe that the impossible is possible.

Dive in and explore the infinite range and wonder of life as lived by others and then seek to incorporate their experiences into your own life's story.

#SWEET SUCCESS: Not all models need be taken from history—or be dead for that matter. Spend time with living people and learn of their rich and exciting lives. Make a list of ten great people you want to know who are still alive. Now think through how you can know them. Write them a letter, call them, mail them a present, or send them flowers. Meet them and start a dialogue with them. In my life, I've been surprised that the majority of writers I've reached out to have answered and helped me, including Michael Port, Jeffery Fox, Steve Chandler, Simon Bailey, and Jim Collins. Your list may include your grandfather, Michael Phelps, your Aunt Doreen, Jeff Bezos, Yo-Yo Ma, Gordon Ramsay, Tasuku Honjo, Usain Bolt, Vivienne Westwood, and Isabel Allende.

#SWEET SUCCESS: Now take a look at some dead people. Make a list of ten great historical people. For each of these, endeavor to read as many biographies as possible about them. After five or six biographies, you really start to get a flavor for the person. A list of some of my favorites include Leonardo da Vinci, Alexander the Great, Madame de Staël, Julius Caesar, Napoleon, Beethoven, Goethe, George Washington, Duke Ellington, and Albert Schweitzer.

#AESTHETIC

The "aesthetic" has lost fashion over the last few years. Instead we strive for comfort, utility, quantity, or fashion where ugly is the new beautiful. We rarely consider if something is "beautiful." We may dive into "cute" but skip the overall aesthetic of design, function, and appearance that can elicit an emotional response.

I understand the lack of practicality in wandering around in our daily lives asking, "Is it beautiful," and very few emails or sales meetings will earn the critical acclaim of "Beauty," with a capital "B." But maybe they should. Of all the emails and meetings I have, most are pretty boring. Imagine, if you will, if Hemingway were writing our email or Quentin Tarantino filming our sales call. There would be an aesthetic there and we would think in a larger way not just about ourselves, but their relation to the receiver and the nexus they create.

What I'm suggesting, though, is that you become aware of the aesthetic in your life. Perhaps start by being a viewer and jumping into a museum or listening to a bit of Berlioz or Dvořák, or maybe Duke Ellington or Benny Goodman is more your style (check out Benny Goodman's commissioned work "Contrasts" composed by Bartók and performed by Szigeti, Goodman, and Bartók—it's mind-bogglingly amazing). Even more simply, walk outside and look through your town at the architecture or the forest and the shape of the trees for aesthetic qualities. John Ruskin felt the two were not exclusive and could find much beauty in the world. Here are two of my favorite Ruskin quotes:

> "Remember that the most beautiful things in the world are the most useless; peacocks and lilies for instance."

> "Summer is delicious, rain is refreshing, wind braces up, snow is exhilarating; there is no such thing as bad weather, only different kinds of good weather."

When I studied negotiation skills, I had an excellent teacher who taught that the environment was controlled by the expert negotiator—the temperature can make the person feel uncomfortably hot or cold or mild, if the end met your needs. You moved the chairs, arranged the clock, put people where you wanted them to go. In short, control the environment and time to the best of your ability.

Thinking about the aesthetic is much the same. You can control how you feel. You can control your desk, what's on it, what's on the wall, the color of the wall, and the color of your pen. You control the cup you use to drink your tea, the clothes you put on your body, and the case you slip over your smartphone. Are you selecting the "aesthetic"? Again, we often select to choose the "cool" or "fashionable" or "cheapest" or "most expensive" rather than a piece of beauty.

Contrary to how most of us live, life is finite, unless you're a vampire, in which case you'll live a couple of thousand years in a melancholic state and then end up with a stake through your chest. So relatively speaking, vampire or mortal, in a few short years, only a handful of hours, you will die. Regardless of your belief in the afterlife, your time and the world that you know will be "boundless and bare/The lone and level sands stretch far away," as Shelley told us. To live in an ugly world is a shame. Start to create the aesthetic. You may not have the money or time to redo a room, but small things can give simple pleasure. Look for ways to make your world more aesthetic, be it a desk, email, closet, shelf, wall, anything around you.

When I was very poor, I could find something from the dollar store and use a bit of imagination, take a small shelf and put quotes and pictures that made the dull white come alive and make me smile. With a few added moments and attention to my environment, the world contained just a sliver more beauty that could spread further into my life.

#SWEET SUCCESS: In your commonplace book ask yourself, "What is beauty?" Can you find twenty-five beautiful things? What things can you start making more beautiful in your life? When you write a report at work, do you feel the beauty in your words and the flow of the sentences? When you make a sales presentation, do your PowerPoint slides have an aesthetic quality of art? Beauty creates passion; passion creates belief in what you are doing and opens up possibilities and new ways of seeing the world. In what ways can you make your world a more beautiful place?

This week, commit to one aesthetic act.

#MISTAKES

It's an old adage that what we fear is the unknown. We like to have answers and know the right way, but we fear being wrong. It's natural, as we are taught right from wrong from childhood to help us enter society and live a well-adjusted life. Then in school, we are tested to make sure we are learning the lessons correctly and, again, mistakes are pointed out.

By the time we reach adulthood, we are stuck in the "how to" realm of searching for the right way of doing things, with an embedded fear of being wrong. It might be liberating and frightening to realize that there are no answers. In six thousand years, things that have been wrong for some were okay for others—humans are wired to be pragmatic. In Egypt, it was okay for siblings to marry and have families; after the Thirty-Years War, it was a necessity that the few men took more than one wife to continue the society; and in New Guinea, to celebrate the death of a warrior and help them into the afterlife, cannibalism was allowed. These are extreme, but in a variety of small ways on a daily basis, things may be taboo for your neighbor and vice versa.

When we start to mix with others on a daily basis, we find that some methods may be better than others. That's what makes doing it yourself—DIY—so popular, whether you're building a deck, learning how to raise and breed goldfish, practicing scales so that you can learn to play Mozart's clarinet concerto, or taking art classes to copy the masters and learn style and technique. At work, we read time management books and learn how to shut off email, take a sales class to negotiate a contract, and learn to create an outline for a novel. Right answers and having a "how to" can help you learn and hone in on a skill.

But be wary of right answers. Learn to try new things and embrace mistakes. Be wary of books that will guarantee the ability to lead you to happiness, develop your personality to meet your spouse in twelve weeks, get rich quick, or give you the fourteen habits that will lead to ultimate success. These books may inspire you and make you feel good, but as you go through and start to read biographies, you realize there are no rules, rarely absolutes, and just because something works one way does not mean that it cannot work another.

Many entrepreneurs and artists are self-taught. Take a look at some famous guitar players who taught themselves: Brian May, Jimi Hendrix, Slash, Joe Perry, Mike Cambell, and B.B. King. And the more you read about others, you find that they took a lesson or two or spoke to others around them, but it was trying, playing, failing, and having fun in the process that made them the musicians they became, not any sort of lessons or how-to.

Jean Cocteau, one of my favorite artists, writers, and filmmakers, is well known for his magically surreal version of *Beauty and the Beast* (in my opinion, much better than the Disney version; plus it's in French, and French is such a sexy language). Many of the effects are so magical simply because Cocteau had no idea "how" to "correctly" make a movie. He invented ways that worked for him. The same holds true for the magic that gave us *Star Wars*. George Lucas had to create many of the special effects, sounds, and visions because nothing was available.

Leonardo da Vinci (April 15, 1452–May 2, 1519) was born in Vinci, near Florence and died in Amos, France at age sixty-seven. We know him for his Mona Lisa and The Last Supper. Leonardo da Vinci is unequaled in history as someone who discovered the world, directly looked at it passionately, and questioned the status quo. He was skilled and classically trained, but no "how to" stood in his way of discovery. He was incessantly interested in inventions, painting, sculpting, architecture, science, music, mathematics, engineering, anatomy, geology, astronomy, and history.

He was born to a lawyer, Piero da Vinci, from a peasant woman, Caterina. He grew up around art and was educated by the famous Verrocchio. He lived at a time when he knew such titans as Michelangelo and Raphael and served under the Medici and died in the service of Frances I of France.

He grew up with his mother in Anchiano, a delightful little Tuscan town near the river Serchio, surrounded by fields of green. At age five he moved to his father's home and lived in the town of nearby Vinci. His father married four women and he had twelve younger siblings.

At the age of fourteen, Leonardo went to work as an apprentice to Verroccio—one of the finest Florentine artists of the day. In Verroccio's studio, he would meet other great artists and learn the skills of drawing, painting, and sculpting, along with other necessary skills such as carpentry and mechanics. The artists of the Renaissance were like the Hollywood stars of today.

In his late 20s, he started to receive commissions to paint altar pieces for chapels, but like so much of what Leonardo worked on, he left them unfinished. He had to move to Milan where he worked for the famous house of Sforza. Some of his best work was done there, such as the *Virgin of the Rocks* and *The Last Supper*.

When he was 50, he worked for Cesare Borgia as a military engineer and mapmaker. After a couple of years, he returned to Florence and then Milan. In his 60s, he was employed by the Medici Pope, Leo X, helping to work on the Vatican with Raphael and Michelangelo.

He finally moved to France under the patronage of Francis I, where he was given the freedom to work as he pleased.

The reason to study Leonardo da Vinci is to see what a human is capable of. We can learn from his ability to find interest in everything around him, to reach out to the world and capture it in art or just in drawing, and to have a curiosity of the universe that never ceased. In his paintings, we can see the depth of his feeling and the precision of his craft, and in his notebooks the variety of his skill and technique and imagination.

#SWEET SUCCESS: Start exploring how to incorporate more ways to do things in your own way. Don't worry about the "how to" to develop your personality, get rich quick, think like a millionaire, win friends, and learn the habits of success. Dump them. They are a crutch for those who lack creativity (and have forgotten to study character—see #Biographies). If you want to do something, visualize it and give it a try. As Miles Davis, the jazz genius, said, "Do not fear mistakes, there are none." There are no mistakes, just outcomes. Make the outcomes you want. When you don't know how to proceed, be creative. Necessity is the mother of ingenuity. Even Shakespeare spelled his name eight different ways. Forget the "how to" and move on to "you can do."

#GREETINGS

When my son graduated from high school, the teachers asked the students to write "thank you" cards to their parents or guardians. When my wife and I received ours in the mail, we were touched. Only four sentences in length, it was appreciative and warm. It now hangs on the wall.

I might be "old school" and out of vogue, but I still love to handwrite "thank you" notes. It only takes a few moments more than an email, but the impact is much stronger. I try to take the time to think a bit more than I do when dashing off a few lines of text in an email. I may write basically the same thing, but the message received is different than the message in the inbox.

By you being the change—personifying the change you wish to witness in others—you inspire others and, in turn, inspire yourself. Just to take the time and handwrite something will slow down your thoughts and deepen them. When someone goes to their mailbox, they generally expect only machine-automated pieces of "junk"—bills and advertisements. Here is a chance for you to open up the world to others wherever you live—in the same city or the same house or the other side of the world. My wife loves to receive a love note in the mail!

Often when people receive postcards, they will be hung on the fridge. At minimum, they will be received with a smile. What a great way to spread joy in someone's life.

#SWEET SUCCESS: Go out and buy five postcards, then head off to a coffee shop and buy yourself your favorite beverage. Take the postcards out and write a few simple lines to someone you would love to hear from. Keep it light, simple, quick, and easy. This is one of my favorite exercises. Out of the postcards I send, often the replies are filled with wonder and joy that I've spent the time and effort to write out a card.

#WALKING

Take a walk. If for no other reason, you will become healthier and that should be a good enough reason on its own. If, however, you're one of those skeptical people who enjoy being persuaded, then read on.

When you take a stroll, your heart beats faster, increasing the blood flow that will easily strengthen your heart and lungs. Your legs and core strengthen. Your breath deepens, and when this happens more oxygen flows to your brain, and this in turn will increase the ideas you'll have when you're writing in your commonplace. So, let's see—good body, smarter, no downside. Perhaps a good idea.

It is no wonder that some of the greatest thinkers and leaders of all time were walkers. The eminent German philosopher, Immanuel Kant, was known by everyone in Heidelberg to take walks along the Philosopher's Way—they could set their watch by his regularity, but could make neither heads nor tails of his writing that was as difficult and winding as a mountain trail.

Ralph Waldo Emerson too walked miles to retrieve his mail. He was also acquainted with the great American naturalist, John Muir, who wandered through the forests and was insightful enough to bring along his friend, Teddy Roosevelt, who also loved a vigorous hike. Together, they set up the National Forrest Service and protected much of the natural splendor in the U.S.

If you would like to meditate when you walk, explore the walking meditation that Ram Dass taught. You focus attention to each movement of a step; the sole, heel leaving the ground and then returning to the ground, in a slow, rhythmic patter. The slower the better, mindful in each movement, like a sloth crawling in the branches of a cecropia tree.

Some walk for health. Others think of all the blessings in their life, while someone else may love to walk with others and have a deep dialogue.

There was a study done with runners, but I'm sure the results would hold true for walkers as well. The study looked at how brain cells fired for runners who were on treadmills inside versus runners who were outside. The ones who ran outdoors proved to be more creative. Along with the physical, the constant, changing sensory input increased the synaptic firing and building of gray matter.

#SWEET SUCCESS: This week, look to take a good thirty-minute walk. Then try to squeeze in two fifteen-minute walks. Sample different times of the day. Of course, lunchtime, but maybe before work or after dinner. Mix it up and see what works best for you.

#NAMES

We often see ourselves in only one way. We build stories around names and titles; some of them are good, some not so good. Some of the stories were handed down to us. You may know the history of your name. Telling that story so often has reinforced the content. If you were named "Francisco," you would have a name of Spanish origin. Some people may call you Francis for short. Maybe Francis or Little Frannie. You would have told people that the origin of the name means "free one." The name may have come down through the family and a distant relative may share that name and their stories may be part of your historical makeup. Maybe you got into a fight or two when called Little Frannie and are insistent in being called Francisco without exception. The point here is that we tie history, story, and myth together around our name. Rarely, if ever, do we question that and step out of the confines of that name.

Your parents named you, but you don't have to keep that name. Hippies used to give themselves new wonderful names like Moonbeam, Jazz Diamond, and Bob.

In Japan, using the Japanese alphabet, the spelling for my name is a bit different and I can write my name in two different ways—David as "Dabito" and "Debido" and should be written "Dabido" if I was following the proper spelling that is used for famous people, like David Beckham. Then I found out that the statue Michelangelo carved was the "Dabide" in Japanese—closer to the original Hebrew pronunciation and a unique third pronunciation. I told people I was named after that statue, so I would call myself that pronunciation and spelling.

"But that is only for the historical king and sculpture, not living people," a colleague told me, as he walked away snickering.

When I pronounced my name in this way over the next week, the Japanese corrected me. Through tears of laughter, they told me, "No, that's only for the historical David." It made me examine how I wanted to be regarded and use my name, and how it reflected who I was.

This had happened before. When I was growing up in the early grades of elementary school, kids loved to make fun of my last name, and everyone referred to me as "Sweet." They would tease me and it generally made me upset. Okay, I admit it, I was on the playground crying, bemoaning my horrible surname and all the Sweets who came before me, even going so far as hating candy. Then in sixth grade I got used to it and started to print "SWEET" on all my shirts. I embraced the name. In an ironic turn, everyone soon started calling me "David." So at age ten, I had passed my course in Reverse Psychology 101.

Titles are another way that we label and name ourselves. There is power and authority in being a CEO instead of an Assistant Vice President. I've known Controllers who had more responsibilities than a lot of CFOs, but the CFOs had a certain C-Suite ambiance about them.

You are what you name yourself. A business owner I knew gave himself the job title on his business card as "Chief Enthusiast." It forced him to be enthusiastic all the time! Or a developer called himself a "Rock Star of Development." Or how about the Vice President of Cool, Director of Imagination, or Chief Catalyst. In a Star Wars theme of our office, our marketing department has three levels of marketing professional: Marketing Padawan, Marketing Jedi, and Marketing Jedi Master. When people see the business card of a Marketing Jedi Master they will view them differently than someone who is a Vice President of Marketing.

#SWEET SUCCESS: Give yourself a new name, even if you are just pretending. Jot down some notes as to why you selected the name. What's the story behind the name? How has it shaped your life and how can it go on shaping your life? And while you are at it, give yourself a new job title. Even go a step further and give yourself a title. Seriously, if Mick Jagger, Mr. Sex-Drugs-and-Rock-'n'-Roll can be knighted, then you surely should get some sort of grandiose title. Go ahead, knight yourself.

#POETRY

Oh, shit! Another section on reading and this one on poetry, no less! I know, you're having flashbacks to eighth grade poetry and thinking to yourself, "Poetry is really hard" or maybe, worse yet, "really boring!"

Or maybe you think to yourself simply, in a soft voice, "Hmmm, no," and turn the page.

Hopefully, though, you may read this and think, "Maybe I can read a verse or two and see if it was better than when I was thirteen." Trust me, many things are better than when you were thirteen! Though, granted, some of that poetry your teacher brought out contained gobbledygook and archaic language. And some of the poetry wasn't relevant for a young person. I'm hoping now a few lines here may open you up to the beauty of words and language. Poetry is a high art form mixing the pinnacle of language and image with that of music. Because you use language, you need to read poetry. Just as biographies take us to the heights of human character, poetry takes us to the heights of reasoning, creativity, language, emotions, and thought.

Try Edward Hirsch's *How to Read a Poem* (despite the title, not a "how to" book, per se, but many ways to fall in love) and then Roger Housden's *Ten Poems to Change Your Life*. Both of these books will place you into reality.

It's quite popular to speak about "emotional intelligence" (EQ). What hogwash and a load of crap. I definitely turn my nose into the air in the height of snobbery. Literally, for thousands of years, the arts have been going deeper into the human psyche of EQ than any social scientist ever could. Even outside poetry, consider the delicacy of the second movement of Rachmaninoff's piano concerto, the anguish of Michelangelo's Pietà, the serenity of Monet's Water Lilies, or the sublimity and grandeur of the Sagrada Família by Gaudi. The arts are open to everyone, and appreciating them doesn't require IQ or EQ or any other psychotherapist babbling BS. What poetry and the other arts offer is a chance to dive into emotions and directly into the human spirit. The more we enter into the arts, the more we are in tune with the spirit of the human condition.

Okay, I'll step down from my soapbox now and return to poetry. But I'm going to keep it near, just under my desk here, as I may need it later.

For an exceptional poet, explore Billy Collins (b. March 22, 1941) who writes poetry that is in plain accessible English and still provides profound depth with a strong dose of humor. He served as Poet Laureate of the United States from 2001 to 2003, and he can sell out poetry readings. He is like the rock star of poetry. His books hit the bestseller list and I assume he has made a good living writing poems, which in our day only a handful of poets can brag about. In this day and age, it is excellent to have an artist who is successful, authentic, accessible, sane (though I've not met the man, so I can't attest to this firsthand), and is the best of the United States.

Born in Manhattan to an Irish father and a Canadian mother, he was an only child. He studied in White Plains and received his Masters and Ph.D. in Romantic Poetry from the University of California. Not only a talented artist, but also a smart guy, driven, serious, and ambitious. The beat poets influenced him, and when I read him I hear echoes of Jack Kerouac in his easy style. The difference is he brings a much deeper understanding and adherence to his craft.

His ability to bring poetry to the world beyond his own work is inspirational. He worked with Garrison Keillor on *The Writer's Almanac* and was popular on Keillor's *The Prairie Home Companion*, a U.S. radio show. He also founded "The Mid-Atlantic Review." He has spread the joy of poetry by working with colleges, magazines, and was even a cultural emissary for the State Department.

I like Billy Collins. He is a model for all artists and he shows the depth that art can give to the human condition. He is a humanist in a time when very few of those still exist. He shows us that art need not be difficult to reach the psyche or the soul. He said that his poetry is "suburban, it's domestic, it's middle class, and it's sort of unashamedly that." I would agree with his assessment. And what he has done is to encapsulate poetry of the 21st century from the U.S.

#SWEET SUCCESS: To again dive into poetry, start with contemporary poetry. Go to www.poets.org and sign up for a poem a day and try it for a week. Check out the weekly poem that the United States Poet Laureate, Ted Kooser (2004–2006) selects (www.americanlifeinpoetry.org). And for a variety of poems, www.poetryfoundation.org has poems from authors contemporary and old alike.

I would recommend, just for sheer accessibility and entertainment, along with a deep sense of emotional understanding of the human condition, reading Billy Collins, Ted Kooser, and Mary Oliver. These poets use easy language that is accessible to anyone. They may be simple, but never simplistic.

Then move on and feel the emotion through the centuries with Walt Whitman, Emily Dickinson, and William Carlos Williams. Through the ages, their words still move readers.

And to see that language and culture isn't a barrier, try Pablo Neruda's wonderful "Ode to my Socks."

I'll leave you with Billy Collins's "Introduction to Poetry."

I ask them to take a poem
and hold it up to the light
like a color slide

or press an ear against its hive.

I say drop a mouse into a poem
and watch him probe his way out,

or walk inside the poem's room
and feel the walls for a light switch.

I want them to water ski
across the surface of a poem
waving at the author's name on the shore.

But all they want to do
is tie the poem to a chair with rope
and torture a confession out of it.

They begin beating it with a hose
to find out what it really means.

#ARÊTE

When I was five years old and starting elementary school, Mom too was going back to college. She enrolled in Red Rocks College. However, one day my school was out and she didn't have a babysitter, so she took me to class with her. She warned me, "You need to behave. This is a college. Sit quietly and draw and color in your book."

Before class began, she introduced me to the professor, Dr. William Boast, a stern looking gentleman, with blond, curly hair, a full mustache, red cheeks, and sporting a brown tweed suit and bow tie. He vigorously shook my hand. I sat with Mom at the back of the classroom and colored with my crayons. The professor's booming voice reverberated through the classroom when he asked, "Who knows Winnie the Pooh, please raise your hand." I smiled and raised my hand. None of the other students did. Mom cringed.

"See," Dr. Boast said, "this young man is better educated than the rest of you."

For the next thirty years, he would be my mentor. He and his wife, Mary, lived in Deer Creek Canyon in a house up near the mesa, with the same gorgeous rock formations that made Red Rocks Amphitheatre. At Christmastime, he and his family would cut down the largest tree they could find and erect it in their home where they had an open two-story space where the tree could stand. It was grand and mighty. The Boasts would open their house to students, friends, artists, and the most unique and wonderful people. One woman was a mystic and could read previous lives. One man, Jim Turner, which happened to be the same name as the Denver Broncos kicker, making it easy to remember his name, played J.S. Bach and Mozart on crystal wine glasses filled with water. He could also play classical music on a saw, as well as differently tuned wrenches. Always a creative circle.

On Sunday nights, Dr. Boast held a class to study history. First it was Arnold Toynbee's long history. Then he started the *Story of Civilization* by Will Durant. At the beginning of the evening, he would spend forty-five minutes or so going through current events and their importance in world history of the past 6,000 years or so. Then we would dive into Rome, medieval Paris, the Italian Renaissance, or the battles of Napoleon.

As I got older, there were more times around the large round table, and it went from just Sunday night to Saturday afternoon when Bill had a class to discuss philosophy. When I started junior high, Mary helped me with spelling, which I was horrible at, and also grammar. In university, I was invited to join the men's group that met once a month and drank single-malt Scotch, smoked cigars, and studied great men in history. Mary ran a similar group for women. We studied great people who could model *arête* for us to aspire to in our life to create a Golden Chain of humanity. Here again was a meritocracy; a chance to learn and find out our ability and talents. Through history, I found, there had always been great people who fulfilled their talent. Some were great artists, like Michelangelo and Picasso; others made money, like the Medici, Fugurs, and Rothschilds. Others were warriors, like Alexander, Napoleon, and Bill's favorite, the Duke of Urbino, who never lost a battle.

Dr. Boast gave me, and everyone who surrounded him, grounding in living in humanism and passion and working on our *arête*. That the liberal arts and learning was divine and contained the fire of life, the fire of the belly, and the fire of curiosity. Life was art, no matter the subject. Whether you worked in marketing, real estate, as a translator, salesperson, composer of music, jewelry maker, or were a fortuneteller, all of those things contained life and provided unique human choices. We were all filled with possibility, infinite potential. If we did what was in the mind of the heart, we could live our art. We had to rise above animals. If we only found comfort in collecting money, we were no better than a chimpanzee that collected sticks. He believed in the humanism of Giovanni Pico della Mirandola:

> A sacred pride should grip us of not being satisfied with the mediocre but to strive (for we can do it, if we want to) with the exertion of all our strength to attain the highest. Let us scorn what is of the earth, let us ignore what is of heaven, let us leave absolutely everything worldly behind us in order to hasten to the abode out of this world, in the proximity of the sublime deity. We do not need to think of stepping back. Of being satisfied with second rank, let us strive for dignity and glory. To attain the highest.

Again, this humanistic thought can be expressed beautifully by the Bard in *Hamlet*:

> What a piece of work is man,
> How noble in reason, how infinite in faculty,
> In form and moving how express and admirable,
> In action how like an Angel,
> In apprehension how like a god,
> The beauty of the world,
> The paragon of animals.

We could argue much about what Hamlet is saying here, and I'll refrain from doing any literary critique, but what I take away is that humans may be only dust, but from dust, how like angels humans can reach. Bill would like that, I think.

Bill hated the beliefs of positivism and the now widespread belief in the mechanical, "how to" methodology when applied to the human condition. He had exceptional respect for the mechanical to start his car, warm his house in winter (he hated the cold), and put a man on the moon, but to resort to the mechanical for endeavors that involved the human, such as managing a sales team, creating a painting, raising a child, or educating kids in a class, he felt best left to the mastery of the human—creativity, mastery of subject, passion, potential, synergy, understanding of context, and love. The creative possibilities of the individual were endless, never based on a "how to" program. He knew that each of us was filled with limitless possibilities to create the world.

As Bill wrote in his autobiography, *Seminalia I: The Omnific Journey*:

> From the beginning it all went to this end I was seeking—no understanding, no goal, no strategy. Had I had, even had those, I would have missed all the joy, all the beauty,

all the wisdom, all the adventures of the mind and heart and body and soul. These all came alive and clean when I never looked for them, never expected them—but I often saw something coming with the music, for I had been making music, art, the sacred in the acceptance of the moments I had been given—had been given to see what I would then create—had been generated so that I might create new art, new life.

#SWEET SUCCESS: Let's look at the *arête*. In your commonplace, write for twenty minutes about excellence. What is it? Who exemplifies it? How can you learn more about it? What can you do to expand *arête* into your life?

#1%

From the get-go, life starts off about following directions. You were born, raised, went to the schools you were told to go to, maybe even studied what you were told to study. Perhaps you needed to take a job that was your second or third choice. Maybe you just ended up doing what you're doing by chance.

There are parts of life that organically expand and open up to us in ways that are wonderful and unexpected. Parents, guardians, loved ones, friends, all have the best intentions for us. They guide us when young to where they believe we have the best chance for success. And over time, you may believe what someone has told you, though you may also change, learn, grow, and understand yourself very differently through time.

No matter your age now, it's never too late to go back and create your own life. The small shifts you make today can later dramatically change the projection of your life. In space, the smallest change in a trajectory can have massive changes in the projection of the spacecraft after it travels further and further out. A one percent change shifts a vessel thousands of kilometers off course. Imagine that for a second—the voyager craft, zooming out past the moon, Mars, continuing out toward Jupiter, Saturn, even further to Pluto, and then some guy at NASA pipes up to his supervisor, "Sorry, I think I'm one percent off in my calculations."

First, there would be a moment of silence. Sheer disbelief. Then chaos would reign supreme, lost jobs, and ruined careers.

You can make the same shift in your life—hopefully at one percent toward the good. A one percent change can move your whole projection out as you go through time. Maybe that one percent change may only make a small difference this week or this month, but continuing on the same path day after day for years makes a huge difference.

When I was in elementary school, I was terrible at sports. By the time I hit junior high, I had totally given up that I would do any sort of sports in my life. In school at sports day, I was the kid given the pea-green colored ribbon that read, "Good Sportsmanship." Then going into my 30s, fat and out of shape, I taught in a high school and needed to do some sort of extracurricular activity with the students, so I thought I'd participate in the class half-marathon.

The first time I went out, I went for a run-walk-run of fifteen minutes. Afterward, exhausted, I collapsed down into my living room as pale as a sheet. But day after day, I persisted in running and soon worked my way up into running races. To date, the furthest I ever ran is a 100K race, but it's early days and my projection may be to head further and further out into the running universe! I still give people a second glance when they say, "He's athletic," and I realize they are talking about me. It's just one of those things I would have never expected in my life because, when I was young, I didn't possess the confidence nor the drive to practice, which I found when I was older. It was that 1 percent change. And who knows, one of these days I could be on SpaceX eating Ben and Jerry's.

#SWEET SUCCESS: If you had your life to live over again, what would you do for a living? Write down ten things you would love to do. Would you be an architect? A rock musician, movie director, monk, biker, biologist, trapeze artist, astronaut? Write down in your CB anything you imagine that you would like to do. Now go through them and try to incorporate one of these back into your life. If you wanted to be a biker, maybe rent a Harley Davidson for the weekend. Maybe pull an Evel Knievel and visit the Grand Canyon. Or if you wanted to be a monk, take a two-day retreat in the mountains. Maybe even just a small thing, like buying a goldfish, could cause a massive shift in your life. I love goldfish.

#EULOGY

Gandhi said, "Live as if you were to die tomorrow. Learn as if you were to live forever." With such an eye on the end-game, so to speak, seeing yourself dead, you start to cherish the living present. There is something that awakens within you when you move into realizing the finite aspect of your life. As you ponder morality, you begin to have a sense of purpose, like a destination. We all end up dead; the path to how we arrive is important. And you realize that if you're having a bad day, it's better than being dead.

One of the great aspects of reading Homer's *The Iliad* is that the hero Achilles has a choice—he can return home, marry a sexy wife, have a beautiful family, live a happy long life, and die unknown; alternatively, he can fight the Trojans and die soon, but his glory will live forever. Achilles had the choice of live "happily ever after" or win glory. As his mother was a goddess with a bit of insider trading knowledge, Achilles knew the end of the story. A choice like this gives us pause to ponder—which would we actually choose? A safe, long life, or a short one of success and fame? Which would you choose?

The Fates in Greek mythology, the Moirai, were three women who decided the length of each person's life. Clotho spun the string of life; Lachesis measured out the string of each person; and Atropos cut the string for the end of life. What a wonderful image. You have a finite amount of string measured out. But what we do with that finite amount of time is important.

Take time to imagine the end of your story. Or many ends, choices, like Achilles. When someone stands up and speaks about you at your funeral, what would you like them to say about you? Who would be saying it? You have a chance to describe your actions and character. As Dr. Boast used to tell me, "Who you are to be, you are now being."

In history, one of the models who was able to live each day like it was his last was Cicero.

Marcus Tullius Cicero (106–43 BC) was a Roman politician, lawyer, and philosopher. In a time of generals and revolutions, he proved that the pen was mightier than the sword. And whether you know it or not, he influenced much of how you learned to write in school, the Constitution of the United States, and the forming of many other governments. And though he lived in the age of Julius Caesar where time has helped fade facts, we owe to Cicero the preservation of history—the knowledge of the lives and times of Rome during a turbulent transition from republic to empire.

Cicero was a self-made man. Though he came from a wealthy family, he was outside of the normal aristocratic ruling class. He chose a life as a lawyer where he could make political connections and learn public speaking (his record of how he mastered speaking influenced speakers and writers in Europe and the U.S. until the 20th century, when Latin stopped being widely studied). He was a lawyer of merit and ability. Politically, he was ambitious, and step by step he held different political offices until reaching that of

Consul, the highest Roman office, in the year 63 BC. During his consulship, he saved the republic from a conspiracy to overthrow the government and won the title *pater patriase*, "father of his country." In his long life, this was his high point.

However, the government was soon taken over by the first Triumvirate, which was made up of Caesar, Pompey, and Crassus. Because Cicero preferred the old republic ruled by laws rather than individuals, he opposed the leaders and was banished. He made his peace with the new rulers, and Caesar, often lenient to those who had opposed him, allowed him to return to Rome in return for his support. Shortly after, when Crassus died, another civil war between Pompey and Caesar ensued and Caesar emerged victorious, seizing control of the government. Cicero was forced out of politics and spent his time writing. After Julius Caesar was assassinated and the government was in disarray, Cicero, though without political position or authority, helped lead the government to order. He mentored for a time Caesar's nephew and heir, Octavian, who would soon become the great Augustus Caesar—possibly the greatest statesman to ever live. The battle for power continued between Caesar's main general, Marc Antony, and his heir, Octavian. A peace was found by the creation of the second Triumvirate with Antony, Lepidus, and Octavian sharing power. To secure their power, they had a prescription to kill their enemies. As Marc Antony hated Cicero, he demanded Cicero be added to the list. Antony's men found Cicero, cut off his head and right hand, and brought it to Antony.

Though a successful political leader who helped rule in a time of some of the greatest people who ever lived, it is as a writer that he had the greatest lasting influence. He was perhaps the greatest rhetorician of his time and his style influenced his writing style.

Latin was the *lingua franca* of Europe for over a thousand years, and Cicero's powerful writing style persisted and his works remained in circulation. His clear, articulate, and emotional writing style influenced the early church, the humanists of the Renaissance, and especially the founding fathers of the United States. From his volumes of letters, we know his thoughts and feelings, and he is one of the most real men of an age from which only cold marble statues stare down. Though it may have been in false modesty that Caesar praised Cicero, he was essentially correct when he said of his accomplishments, "It is more important to have greatly extended the frontiers of the Roman spirit than the frontiers of the Roman Empire."

Cicero embodied a person who directed much of his life. He knew what he wanted and moved toward accomplishing each objective. And like most of us, Cicero was born common, but through vision, hard work, and persistence created a life where any number of great eulogies can be given to him.

#SWEET SUCCESS: Start writing your eulogy. Take the time to say what events you accomplished and what kind of character you were in life. You can even go so far as to imagine who will read the eulogy. What will they write on your tombstone? Just the image of seeing yourself dead makes you realize the importance of being alive. Sometimes when people do this exercise, they have a strong surge of emotions well up in them. Realize that this can happen and be open to the emotions and the experience. Record in your commonplace book how it makes you feel.

#ANSWERS

Having more answers forces you to think outside the box, to think creatively, and to search for alternative solutions that you may neglect. Sometimes, if you're an "A" type personality, you may go with the first answer that pops into your head. You've been trained that actions speak louder than words and you're ready to take action! If a solution presents itself, you move on it. This type of action/reaction lends itself well to those in leadership positions, and for this reason you may find a great deal of success in your life. But you may also feel frustrated with your inability to grow by seeing other sides of an issue.

On the other end of the spectrum, you may be a person who is locked into finding the perfect answer. You may wait and not take any action. You want to find the exact solution for all of life's challenges. You want the correct answer. In this end of the spectrum, rather than action, you're stuck looking for perfection, which leads to inaction.

When you start to see possibilities, whether you tend to find yourself locked into action or inaction, you start to explore how the world works. You start to live creatively and freely. Having the freedom to select different ways of doing things is part of the spice of life. When you have an answer, you close down any other information because you have "all the facts" and you have "the answer" and everything else is a burden to prove you wrong. Or if you believe there is only "the answer"—you are burdened to find that single, correct answer.

When looking back over history, it's easy to smile with a 20/20 vision of the future. At one time we could walk across the town or to the next village and know that indeed the Earth was flat. Then astronomers and sailors started to look for alternative answers because the "facts" told them that the answer was different. Indeed, the Earth was round. The "right" answer, based on facts and a great deal of research, turned out wrong. (In case you are interested, you can still join the Flat Earth Society.) When you know a "fact," it's good to remind yourself that that is based only on historical evidence; the future may turn out to have a different set of facts.

Next time you're faced with a challenge where you need to make a choice, give yourself several. Your initial choice may be the best and you may continue with that, but you'll have confidence that you've searched for other ways of doing something. Take a look at opposites. Most bright ideas come from playing with what you "know." When you have started the process of looking for more and more answers, you'll surprise yourself at the possibilities.

In groups, we often use brainstorming or mind maps to generate ideas, but for individual decisions we ignore the process. When seeking for more answers, you can use the simple questions—who, what, where, why, and how.

And if you would like to organize a problem and solution, look at the five major ways that Aristotle used to organize.

- Define: What are the parts and the purpose?

- Structure: What are the parts?

- Classification: Where does it fit in with others?

- Process: What are the steps?

- Compare and contrast: How is it similar and different to others?

Realizing there are always answers gives you the flexibility to find creative solutions and help coach yourself into different ways of living.

#SWEET SUCCESS: Take a problem you're trying to find the answer for. Set yourself a quotient to come up with five answers. Rephrase the problem and come up with five more answers. Ask yourself, "who, what, where, why, and how." Then go through and define, take the structure, classify, process, and compare/contrast. Make it fun and you'll soon search out chances to find more and more answers.

#ALIENS

When I was five years old, I dug a hole through the planet. Excitedly, running inside, I yelled to my mom, "I dug through the Earth! There are Japs on the other side." I don't know where I had learned the word, "Japs." Probably from a World War II movie on television.

Without skipping a beat, Mom replied, "That's super! And you shouldn't call Japanese people 'Japs.' It's not polite. Plus your great, great, great, great, great grandfather was Japanese."

As a gullible five-year-old, I believed her. In fact, I believed her until college, but from that day stopped using a derogatory term for Japanese. Once you're part of a group, a part of you accepts it.

I loved to rummage around in books, including journals, and would spend time looking over the bookshelves. One book was long and silver—a book to catch an eight year-old's eye. To my surprise, the book was about aliens. An alien had come down to Earth and started to describe the human condition. I later found that the book was for one of Mom's psychology courses, but the impact made me realize that how we see and describe the world paints different pictures.

This exercise will ask you to challenge your assumptions and view your life from outside its current cultural and linguistic context. Culturally, you'll no longer be a nationality but something studied by an alien. Second, as an alien on a scientific research team, you'll lack the day-to-day vocabulary that you are familiar with and will need to describe the things in your world rather than name them.

How would aliens describe your life? Look through the eyes of someone without all the filters of sociology, psychology, and hidden premises that we put on life. When you sit down to a meal, did you intake contents from an animal that was injected with chemicals and coloring then wash it down with a can of colored brown liquid? Did you put an earpiece into your ear and walk around talking to yourself? A bit of a different view to eating a hamburger, sipping a cola, and talking on your mobile phone. What else can you describe from the point of view of an alien? Take yourself to your leader.

#SWEET SUCCESS: Grab your CB and describe a day in your life. Use the bullet points below—and others that you can think of. Imagine yourself as a scientist from another planet. You've come to study this species and your life represents all humans. Describe what you see. And don't take for granted that you know what anything is called.

- What did you do when you woke up?

- What foods did you eat?

- What toiletry habits do you have?

- Who do you speak to? What tones of voice?

- How do you travel?
- Where do you go?
- Who do you meet?
- What rituals do you have?
- What similarities to others do you see? Differences?
- Are there activities that resemble games?
- Are there activities that resemble what other animals do?

#WHAT IF

Just by asking, "What if?" you push limits, challenge beliefs, and create possibilities. What if your hair was blue? What if you ate only fish? What if houses had feelings? What if there were no computers? What if dolphins walked? What if humans were the only intelligent beings in the universe?

Play with the idea and have fun! You'll be surprised at how many new ideas you can come up with at work, along with improvement of processes!

As an executive coach, I ask people a series of "what if" questions to help them determine what they want to do with their careers. Because asking the question poses little threat, people are open to start thinking about what would happen if they moved to a new job, had a different job title, if their pay changed. Once the question is asked, "What if you moved to this company as a manager?" then the imagination takes over and possibilities stream in.

When I've used "what if" in arbitration and negotiation, the process has been critical in breaking down barriers and deadlocks. If two people are stuck in a deadlock and start to ask "what if," other possibilities present themselves. Momentum in the negotiation begins to proceed forward. The change first takes place in the imagination and then the belief in possibilities occurs. Without asking "what if" questions, the process can freeze, often resulting in failure.

#SWEET SUCCESS: Take a question you are thinking about and start asking a series of "what if" questions. You don't need to answer the questions, but rather just build more questions around the challenge.

For example, pretend you want a new job. Go through spontaneously asking a series of questions such as:

- What if I retired when I was 75?

- What if I lost my job in a month?

- What if I lived on eating peanut butter sandwiches only?

- What if I outsourced my job?

- What if computers did my job for me?

- What if I was doing my ideal job, what would I be doing?

- What if I worked 100 hours a week and loved it, what would I be doing?

There are no limits to the range of questions. And then when you start to go back and answer these questions, think laterally, creatively, pushing the envelope to the common questions and answers you might currently ask yourself.

#SWEET SUCCESS: For the next week, each day, ask yourself 20 "what if" questions. Your first day might be, "What if I did this, what subjects would I question?"

#GARDENING

Ahh, to touch the soft dirt and feel the leaves and plants, to smell soil and greenery! In our city-living, suburban lives, gardening helps root us back to the earth—literally. We find that we are part of the earth—our bodies are the earth of us, as compared to the mind and the spirit. In addition, we learn from the example of the earth how to cultivate, nurture, and nature our world and our lives. I'm not trying to go all hippie, tree-hugger, new age on you. But there is an importance to staying connected to the soil and our relationship to it, our mastery over it, and even bringing it to an art form. Check out English gardens and elegant bonsai for example.

Understanding this power and our relationship to it is important for our survival. We have the power to shape the earth and all that is on it (and of course, a huge responsibility, which we're not doing well at). We learn how fragile plants are and how quickly they fade, wilt, and die without the proper care. Watching the green leaves fade to brown and wondering what has happened connects us to the world of farming and where our food originates. It's easy to take for granted the food we digest and how many centuries we've put into learning how to toil the soil. Now, with the advent of hearty insecticides and pesticides, as well as greenhouses and genetic engineering making our plants heartier, the ability to eat certain fruits and vegetables year-round and feed a population of the planet on a scale never before imagined is significant. All this you can touch in the earth when you pot some pansies or try to grow basil on your balcony.

My grandfather had a flower shop; the green-thumb gene seems to have skipped me, however, though it gave me an awareness of gardening. When I had a house, I did okay with some tulips and planted two roses; one of them lived. I've since found my gardening solace in philodendrons; they are a forgiving plant. You can snip off a branch, throw it in a glass of water and watch the roots sprout. Then planting it in dirt, the long green vines sprawl out with shiny green leaves. Currently, I live in the most crowded city on the planet on the 35th floor. And for someone who lacks horticultural sense, a small pot on a balcony is a big enough plot for me to garden. In a pot, I have pansies in the spring and summer and they do well, braving the strong winds we sometimes have. In summer as well, I may work with some herbs, which I like because they are pragmatic, I.e., I can eat them. The basil also finds its way into salads and pastas.

You need not get fancy with gardening. However, I do encourage you to get a plant and care for it. It's not about becoming a horticulturist or trying to move you to the farm. I'm not telling you to be a vegan or only eat organic. If that's your cup of tea (herb tea, I would presume) then go for it. But I'm looking to start with the simple—touch the earth and be a part of it, even if it's in a small way. As a human in today's busy age, in an age when it is mainly about the self and we touch our mobile phones more than our children, it is good to connect to the planet. This can be challenging in the concrete jungle. Also, this exercise helps you to look outside yourself and care for something unconditionally by helping it flourish. It may die. Strange to say, but that's life.

#GARDENING

You'll need to hold on to both of those outcomes. This gives you a chance with only a small amount of time to reach out into the world and care for it and try to raise it.

#SWEET SUCCESS: Get a plant. Go as wild or as simple as you wish. Or better still, plant some seeds in a pot. In the store, you may find many types of greenery that you neglected, and feel enticed to go with a cactus or potted plant. Go for it! Take a chance and learn to garden, even on the smallest of scales. Gardening gives you a chance to clear weeds and grow. This also happens in your mind.

#ANGEL'S ADVOCATE

As Marci Segal points out, an angel's advocate is someone who sees what's good in an idea and supports it. We all know how to help out by playing the "devil's advocate"—we generally sound out the shortcomings of an idea. The term is a euphemism for skeptics to critique. Don't be fooled. The quickest way to kill an idea is by playing the devil's advocate.

When you hear a new idea, be an "angel's advocate" and find ways to promote and build the idea. Challenge your teams to have angel's advocates where they find at least three good reasons why a new idea will work before the devil's advocate starts to speak.

This may sound much easier than it is. Psychologically speaking, some people are just wired to find troubles with any idea. When we lived in caves and hunted mammoths, humans needed a good dose of skepticism to stay alive. Trying a new cave or a different hunting ground could kill you and the rest of the tribe. And nothing can die quicker than a new idea.

New ideas need protecting. New ideas are like seedlings, and a harsh word, sometimes even the smallest raised eyebrow or the unbelieving sigh, mows down an idea in an instant. When you spend a moment protecting the idea and building reasons why something will work or can improve, the new idea gains momentum. The idea grows, expands, develops, and blooms. With each idea, new possibilities occur.

#SWEET SUCCESS: Help an idea become a reality. Stop for a moment and think of three reasons why it will work or how to improve an idea before describing why something won't work. Tell others what you're doing and ask for their help in doing it too. Also, give the caveat that the devil's advocate can always have a chance, but the angel gets the first turn. You'll find that positive ideas will catch on, expand, and illuminate from you and around you and your team. It's a great way to earn your wings and enter the heaven of creative thinking.

#HUMOR

One Sunday, I was golfing with my wife. She asked me, "If I died, would you get married again?"

I was surprised she asked me this. Shocked, I answered, "No, my love, I wouldn't."

But she persisted, "I'm sure you would."

So I finally relented and responded, "Okay, maybe I would."

Then she asked me, "Would you let her sleep in our bed?"

At this, I replied, "Yes, I guess so."

Then my wife asked, "Would you let her use my golf clubs?"

And I replied, "No, she's left-handed."

Pow!

What is the funniest thing you've done in the last year? What did you learn? Humor gives you a perspective on life. Sometimes from your mistakes, with the hindsight of time, the humor of the event can teach you a lot. Granted, for some events, especially that one night from college, it may take a lot of time and a lot of hindsight. Find humor in your past, make light of it, and learn from it.

Humor has been found to release dopamine into the brain when you laugh. For that reason, movies, stories, or just hanging out with people who make you laugh will physically, as well as psychologically, make you healthier.

Research repeatedly tells us how important laughter can be. Andrew Osawald recruited students and had them watch funny movies and found that participants were able to perform some math problems better than a control group. When you make something funny, you can be more productive, produce better work, find yourself less distracted, and even enhance your memory. In *Social Psychology Quarterly*, researchers O'Quinn and Aronoff pointed out that humor will also get buyers to pay more. They found that when the salesperson—either a woman or a man—used jokes and other humor, the buyer—again, either a woman or man—would pay a higher price.

There are many studies that show the benefits of laughter in healing an illness, the ability for the body to combat flu, and even cancer. The University of Maryland Medical Center in Baltimore found that laughter helps prevent heart disease. And if you're already healthy, making things funny will help reduce stress, you'll feel more relaxed and sleep better, which also contributes to a healthy lifestyle.

Bottom line: don't be a sourpuss.

As one of the greatest comedians to walk the planet, Red Skelton, said, "Live by this credo: have a little laugh at life and look around you for happiness instead of sadness. Laughter has always brought me out of unhappy situations."

Which reminds me of a time that I walked into this zoo. The only animal in the zoo was a dog. It was a Shih Tzu.

Admit it, you laughed.

#SWEET SUCCESS: Make sure to laugh once a day. Have a big chuckle. Go out of your way to find something funny to laugh about. Search out a comic on the Internet and watch until you laugh out loud. Intentionally add comedy to your life. Perhaps there is a movie that you've been meaning to watch; try and find it and watch it.

#SWEET SUCCESS: This week, when you speak to someone, ask who is their favorite comedian. After finding out the name, watch a clip of the comedian on YouTube.

#SWEET SUCCESS: At least once this week, ask someone to tell you a joke. From ages 5 to 105, people generally know one or two jokes and search for the time to tell them. You can give them that opportunity.

#SWEET SUCCESS: In your CB, write down the funniest thing that has ever happened to you in your life. Who was there? What were the circumstances? What made it funny? Don't worry about trying to make your writing funny. The point is to remember and just enjoy writing and remembering one of the funniest times in your life.

#INNOCENTS ABROAD

When you leave the security of your home or the rhythm of you daily life and enter into vacation, many things change. You need to search out the basics, even if you've been on bookings.com and made all the necessary arrangements. You find yourself in a strange bed, meeting new people, seeking out edible food. You see things that are new and unique. If you've gone to a foreign country, there may be a good chance to try and learn to communicate with the natives.

Finding yourself in such a situation is a great opportunity to write down your observations and feelings. They will be new and unique and put you on edge. You'll discover something about the place you're visiting, and by writing you'll learn about yourself. Look around you and see what you can implement into your business and private life. When you travel, whether it is to the local ski town or beach, or to Bora Bora or Paris, you will begin to see things differently. When you return home, you will also begin to see your own place with new eyes. Once, when I was hitchhiking in Ireland, I hitched a ride from a potato farmer who had been to Dublin once; other than that, he had never left his town. His world and way of doing things were very different from mine. First, it was amazing to me that we were both speaking English, as I could only understand half of what he spoke. I was also amazed that he had lived his life in such a small area, when all I wanted to do was explore the world. It was amazing to see life through his experience. I was so innocent.

Though Disney got us to start singing that this is a small world, we can sometimes appreciate that it is also a big one. As James Joyce wrote, "Every life is many days, day after day. We walk through ourselves meeting robbers, ghosts, giants, old men, young men, wives, widows, brothers-in-love. But always meeting ourselves." When you travel, even just down the street, the sights, sounds, and smells can open up this small world to the very eclectic world it is.

#SWEET SUCCESS: Take your commonplace book with you on vacation. Maybe it's just a weekend away. Write down the sounds and sights, what you eat, people you meet, places you go, names of things. Write down what you miss from home. Write down what you don't miss. Write down the random thoughts that pass through your mind. Everything and anything—just set aside fifteen minutes each day of your vacation and jot down some thoughts. You will have made yourself an excellent souvenir for your trip.

#ASTRONAUT

The song from T-Bone Burnett, "Humans from Earth" always sparked my imagination with the switch that the humans were the invading aliens:

> *We come from a blue planet light-years away*
> *Where everything multiplies at an amazing rate*
> *We're out here in the universe buying real estate*
> *Hope we haven't gotten here too late*
> *We're humans from earth*
> *We're humans from earth*
> *You have nothing at all to fear*
> *I think we're gonna like it here*

Then, growing up, I loved reading Ray Bradbury's *The Martian Chronicles*. And like many of my generation, *Star Wars* enamored me with space and the adventures "a long time ago in a galaxy far, far away." I remember the spark in my son's eye when asking him what he wanted to be when he grew up and he answered, "A spaceman."

However, many of us abandon the dream in adulthood. Reality crashes in. We earn a "D" in Mrs. Steinbeck's math class and fail Dr. Atkinson's physics. Parents and teachers try to guide you into more manageable career paths. Or you may find that every time you board an airplane, you need a barf bag.

Regardless, the wonderful thing about your commonplace book is that it frees you to visit the icy clutches of space without fear of death, vomit, or the need to do calculus. You can go into it and write any crazy thing you want. You can list your five-year voyage as the captain of a spaceship. You can go through and again imagine what it was like to live your childhood dream, no matter what it was—tap dancing, movie star, Franciscan monk, firefighter, actor, rock and roll guitar player, chef, mad scientist, superhero (particularly Green Lantern), jewelry designer, architect, botanist, or Olympic swimmer. All those professions, at least in your imagination, are open to you.

The imagination is a powerful tool. It's good to practice using it. If you go through and imagine what you are doing, you can then take small aspects of your imagined self and put them into your life.

If you have the dream to be an Olympic swimmer, maybe now is the chance to write a bit about it and take a small action. Is there a pool near your home? Maybe time for a new swimsuit.

Or do you still crave to dance? Can you go out dancing?

If you wish to act, is there a small local theater group that may need someone? The action need not be a big one. Even purchasing a simple token or spending an hour at the natural history museum and visiting the planetarium might be enough.

Why do we go through and re-visit our childhood dreams? Many of us wander through life ignoring our dreams, ignoring our intentions, failing to reach our potential. This is your one shot at life; there are no others. Henry David Thoreau wrote, "The mass of men lead lives of quiet desperation, and go to the grave with the song still in them." By exploring your childhood dream and finding the smallest aspect of your life that you can incorporate an element or two into helps you crack the veneer of your current life and start to open it up just a bit. That small crack can chip away and give you chances to safely explore new challenges.

One of my friends lived a life selling medical devices and had a dream to play guitar. Though well into his 40s, he took a few lessons. He found a joy in playing flamenco. Soon he started to regularly play and then started to drive his family down to vacations in Mexico. He rekindled a small dream from his childhood and added it to the hustle and bustle to help center himself.

#SWEET SUCCESS: Dare to blast off into a dream! First, take out your CB and set aside ten minutes. Ask yourself, "If I was an astronaut, what would I be doing today?" Now set a timer and write for ten minutes straight. Don't worry about the answer. You may write down, "I have no idea what to write." That's fine, just keep on rewriting that. Eventually you'll tire of that and start to write about fighting aliens, walking on Mars, traveling through another dimension, being sucked into the vacuum of space, or finding the Dagobah system.

Turn the page, and again set the timer for ten minutes. Write what you wanted to be as a child. Let yourself go and realize it is fine to end up writing about the sunshine of the day and how this is stupid and you should be doing work. Expect the resistance and just keep writing. Keep repeating and responding to the phrase, "When I was a kid, I wanted to be an X." Write as many responses as you can. After you complete this writing, go back and quickly read it. Don't judge the writing. You're not expecting to do any great literary masterpiece—this is just free writing and all the grammar and spelling mistakes that you put into your journal are fine. What you are looking for is the kernel of an idea. Is there anything in your writing that resonates from when you were a child that you wish you could recapture? Anything you can take action on?

If not, don't worry. You can come back to this exercise as many times as you like and have as many answers as you want! The more you start to look beyond the boundaries of the one life you have, the more chance you have to create a better life now.

#PEARLY WHITES

Here's a chapter that you can literally sink your teeth into—taking good care of your teeth. Success comes from maintaining health, and health comes from good nutrition. The entrance into the digestive system is your teeth.

I really debated about adding this section, but in the end, I put it in, as I feel it's important to keep ourselves healthy. When I was in elementary school, I had a book that was titled something like *Improve Your Brain*, and it had all kinds of logic puzzles and daily activities to increase the brain's ability to work spatially, logically, creatively, and mathematically. The thing that really struck me in this book was the suggestion in the Introduction to take good care of your teeth.

In my family, my grandparents and aunt all had false teeth. Perhaps this gave me a fear of losing my teeth.

So, for those reasons, I leave this section in the book because it represents not only taking care of your teeth, but all of your physical body—work at it daily, and have regular check-ups.

Teeth, specifically, are one of the most important and easiest parts of the body to maintain. However, if you have pain in your teeth and gums, you'll break down what you're eating. Nutrition suffers, as does your ability to think, create, and maintain health. Your pearly whites are the gateway to good health.

It's as simple as remembering to brush your teeth after every meal. Most Americans I know only brush in the morning and in the evening. In contrast, the Japanese also brush after lunch.

Ask your dentist about the best toothbrush for you. From my experience, the simple ones are much better than the fancy ones that have a strong marketing budget to tell you how good they are. Use soft, up-down strokes and spend the time concentrating on reaching all your teeth. And on a regular basis, change the toothbrush when the bristles begin to fray.

Second, go to the dentist for regular checkups. Preventative cleaning will help maintain healthy teeth and gums and also catch decay prior to becoming serious. A dentist's office is often put on par with torture. But this idea is generally from the childhood horrors we remember of having a cavity or five filled. As an adult, you need to overcome that memory. Maintaining excellent, healthy care of your teeth warrants regular checkups.

If you want to maintain overall health, pay attention to the first and foremost gateway into the rest of the body. I've written about nutrition and exercise and learning; all these start with your ability to digest. Those pearly whites will serve you well.

#SWEET SUCCESS: Invest in a new toothbrush. And if not on the calendar already, schedule your semi-annual checkup.

#IDEAS

Often we get stuck in a rut by the simple act of complacency. We go through our lives the same way day in and day out, rarely questioning what we do or why we do it. The simple patterns and rhythms are important to our life, but small, simple changes can help spice up your life.

This exercise will help you generate new ideas and brainstorm new responses. Pushing yourself to have more and more ideas, even when the first or second idea seems great, will help you see other possibilities. Some possibilities will always be better than others. But your ability to generate new ideas allows you to see potential in nearly any situation, empathize with others because you'll know new ideas come from a variety of sources, and creatively help you open doors that were once closed.

#SWEET SUCCESS: Every day for a week, write down ten new ideas. It doesn't matter what the topic is. The first topic might be, "What ten ideas can I write down?"

1. Places I'd like to visit

2. Anniversary presents for my wife

3. Foods I wish I could cook

4. Animals I'd like to pet

5. Marketing ideas for my company

6. Different ways to answer, "How are you today?"

7. Books I'd like to read

8. Famous sports figures I'd like to meet

9. Ten more ideas for marketing

10. Ways to be more productive

You may find that in the middle of the list, you hit a bit of resistance. That's okay. Keep jotting down ideas. It's okay to put down really terrible ideas! The point is to generate and generate and generate! The more ideas you have, the more opportunities you'll have to find an idea that might change your life. You might even find an idea for the next week to write a list of twenty or thirty ideas for a week! If you write down ten ideas a day, that's seventy a week or around 280 a month—give or take a few days. Just by the sheer number of ideas, you're bound to hit on two or three that catch your fancy and expand how you think, act, and live. Seriously, with 3,650 ideas a year—you're bound to get something to super-charge your world!

#SILENCE

In this exercise, you spend some time quietly with yourself. If you can, spend a whole day alone, in a quiet place. Imagine yourself, for a day, the modern equivalent to Henry David Thoreau, going out into the woods to live deliberately and find quietude. This is difficult to do in this day and age when most of us work and are guided around by our mobile phones and email. As Jean Arp wrote:

> Soon silence will have passed into legend. Man has turned his back on silence. Day after day he invents machines and devices that increase noise and distract humanity from the essence of life, contemplation, meditation… tooting, howling, screeching, booming, crashing, whistling, grinding, and trilling bolster his ego. His anxiety subsides. His inhuman void spreads monstrously like a gray vegetation.

And since Arp's time, the gray vegetation has spread even further. It may be difficult for you to find a whole day, but try to carve out a small portion of time for yourself when you can have quiet alone time.

As our brains are switched on all the time, it's good to give them a chance to relax for a bit. Rather than cramming them with messages, work, forced play, or some sort of media, take the time to just really relax. You're looking for a chance to expose yourself to yourself.

If you're the type of person who enjoys being alone, then this will be easy. Take this time to consciously shut down the talkative side of your brain. Imagine you're a monk or a nun at a convent where there is only silence. The calming effect of this exercise is eye-opening and sometimes profound.

For others it may be difficult and boring. You're used to being connected with others. It may be a challenge for you to stay off the grid. But remember, this is just for a small while, not forever.

There are no correct responses to this exercise. The point is to calm the mind, even for an hour. When you do this, it is like emptying your cup, washing it out, and drying it, ready to again fill it up. If you just keep filling and filling the cup, it soon overflows and you miss the chance to drink and taste. Taking the time to empty yourself allows you the opportunity to fill it with new and fresh ideas.

#SWEET SUCCESS: Find a day and spend it by yourself alone. If a day is too long or not possible, search for a morning or afternoon. And if you can't find this, try to find an hour when you can sit quietly or go out and walk the streets (quiet, back streets). Better yet, find a place in nature to walk, sit, and amble. The point is to let your mind relax. Be alone. What you are searching for in a day of quiet is to find the place the Roman Emperor Marcus Aurelius knew well: "Nowhere can man find a quieter or more untroubled retreat than in his own soul." Don't expect to find earth-shattering awakenings or enlightenment. Don't expect to find anything. Leave expectation at home. All you're doing is giving yourself a mini-vacation so you can go out and see, feel, hear the world, and live outside yourself while being inside yourself without noise. Leave your phone at home. Leave your headphones. Just you and the world.

#NEWS

Imagine two people in a silent room. Perhaps it's a doctor's office. The two are reading magazines. There is a tension. The silence is palpable. Then one person starts to laugh. You can feel the energy change and lighten. The feeling of the room changes and the energy is contagious. Then the person who was laughing shares what they were reading and both people start to laugh. You can imagine the room feeling much brighter. We've all been in a room where someone comes in and the energy of the room brightens.

And of course, the converse is true. There are times too when a certain person enters the room and zaps the energy. Imagine a classroom without a teacher where the students are lively, and then the teacher walks in and the room falls silent.

Watching the news is a bit like having your energy zapped. If the world were a lovely, peaceful place, no one would watch the news because the news would be boring.

"Today on CNN: world peace. Everyone had three square meals and a roof over their head. Across the planet, people helped one another, learned, created, and made a few new discoveries in the world of science. There was also a cure for cancer. And in the weather, a perfect 80 degrees."

CNN would need to start making things up!

The general viewing public likes to watch hardship, tragedy, and troubles—after all, it's the stuff of stories. Because the news needs to capture a viewer's attention, the focus tends to be on floods, bombings, shootings, political intrigue, abuse of power, and other misgivings that this or that country's leader can think of.

Take, for example, the weather. If the weather person came out and said, "Today it will be a sunny, warm day," it would be a bit dull. Rather, "Today there is a chance of rain." The second one will make your animal instinct imagine and prepare for the worst and how to combat the challenge. I've seen it firsthand. When I lived in Florida, where the weather is gorgeous most of the year, the news tended to focus on the horrible weather in the rest of the country. Watching everyone else's bad weather was a Florida pastime.

News, in and of itself, is not an enemy. However, the negative stories are more emotionally compelling and, in turn, promote negative feelings. Many people wake in the morning and watch news that sends out negative energy that weighs them down the rest of the day. Instead of starting the day on a negative, fill that space with positive energy.

In the insightful book *Will It Make the Boat Go Faster?*, Ben Hunt-Davis explains insights about how he and the British rowing team became a team. One of my favorite parts is to have a bullshit filter. Bullshit beliefs create poor performance and make it more difficult to succeed. Much of what we hear on the news is bullshit. To enhance your performance in life, have your own bullshit filter.

#SWEET SUCCESS: Try a news blackout for a week. Fill the time with positive, uplifting, insightful, funny entertainment. Or just leave the news off and see how you naturally fill the time by yourself. Look at what happens when you take a week off from reading newspapers and watching the news. Leave the messages that the media puts out for just one week. What discoveries do you find? How has your thinking changed? What have you missed? So much of the news focuses on trivial information or negative messages that can wear us down. Live light and be happy—turn off the news. After all, people will tell you the important news. People love to share bad news. Create bullshit filters and fill your life with as much positivity as possible.

#TRAVEL

Nothing else will open your mind more than visiting new countries and learning how others live. People all over the world hold many assumptions as true, but after traveling, many preconceived notions disappear. Traveling to exotic places may be an exceptional and wonderful thing to do, but sometimes it may not be financially possible. When this is the case, take mini-vacations in your town. Usually, the place where we live is one of the places we know the least.

Growing up in Denver, rarely did I know many of the places that tourists would come and visit. Only when I made it a priority did I take a mini-vacation and see the botanic gardens, natural art museum, art museum, the Mint, Casa Bonita, and Central City, or take a drive into the mountains or a cruise out into the Eastern Plains. There is so much to do and see in any place. I'll confess that I live in Tokyo, where there are so many things to see and do that traveling becomes almost a non-necessity in order to experience the strange and the exotic.

However, if you have the resources, then prioritize to schedule travel. The time prior to the travel—the anticipation—will focus you. You can read up on where you will go and what you will see. You'll begin to imagine a different place. Of course, during the trip you'll experience all the joy of the travel. And then the afterglow of having created memories and the joy of seeing something new.

If you are the CEO of a company and have more than one office, then pay for your employees to visit other locations. The cross-fertilization of ideas alone will pay for any expenses of the trip and it keeps morale up!

#SWEET SUCCESS: Make a list of twenty places you would like to visit. The list may include the Amalfi Coast, Alaska, a safari in Africa, New Zealand, Capri, Angkor Wat, the Great Barrier Reef, and the used bookstore downtown.

#FENG SHUI

Your life should be beautiful, especially the things around you. Feng Shui, the ancient Chinese philosophy concerning how to create an environment that uses an energy force (ch'i), has moved from being just a spiritual practice to helping create an aesthetic living environment. There are some mystical elements within the philosophy, but what we're concerned with are two of its aspects—aesthetic and functional. The two are often not separate, especially in a well laid-out room or living space. What you're striving for is a way to beautifully design the elements around you—surroundings and living space—in a way that creates beauty in your life. Feng Shui has been doing that for people for thousands of years. With such a long-standing presence in the world, it begs attention.

For example, one idea is to hang a mirror opposite of a doorway. The purpose is to send the bad energy back out the door. I don't worry much about the energy, but what I do like is the relevant aesthetic function of having a mirror opposite a door to provide balance, help open up the space with light, and provide a longer appearance. And when a person walks through the door, they have the experience of seeing themselves. Perhaps all these design elements are what provide the energy; I don't know. But the design advice is solid.

Some of us ignore our living surroundings and just think of where the chair will fit in the room or what color table looks good in the kitchen. However, when you study design and look at a totally different way of designing the space you live in, then you start to pay attention to the world around you. This will send a signal to the brain to help generate a productive life. The interior will replicate the interior of your mind and heart.

If you already think about design, especially for your interior, then fantastic. If you are not aware of Feng Shui, study the main principles of it. There are many good websites and books you can quickly scan through.

One of the joys of life is the creation of that life. Certain aspects we have the ability to control, change, and shape, giving physical manifestation of our mind and spirit. There is no one right way to do this, but Feng Shui gives a beautiful example and is one of the high achievements of the human mind for the creation of space. For me, that is a good way to start.

Your changes may not be large. I find it easiest to start with my desk or a dresser; a whole room overwhelms me. From a desk, I may start to look at the wall and see if I can find a new picture to add. I may then look at the kitchen. What you're looking for are small, easy changes you can incorporate into your home and office. Feng Shui is an ancient art of harnessing the universe's energy. However, like all great things, there is a simple idea at its core—aesthetic beauty. Even if you don't believe in the mystical aspect of Feng Shui, the idea of surrounding yourself with beauty will be a potent way of improving your life.

#SWEET SUCCESS: Find one way to put a bit of beauty into your living space. This may be a single-stem yellow rose on the dining table, a small knick-knack from the dollar store, or some pretty rocks found on a walk you took and sprinkled on a colored plate. Maybe it's hanging a picture you've wanted to hang, purchasing a rug that you've had an eye on, or putting a post card of a Monet "Water Lilies" print on your fridge. The idea is to bring beauty into your life. This week, beautify one space in your life.

#LIBERAL ARTS

The phrase "liberal arts" comes from the Latin *artes liberales*, which means, "worthy of a free person." In classical times, a free person in Greece would study what was needed to take part in a civil life, such as debate and military service. Romans, especially with the help of Cicero, expanded this to include grammar, logic, and rhetoric. The Middle Ages created a curriculum around this that added arithmetic, geometry, music, and astronomy. And in modern times, we added the academic subjects of literature, philosophy, mathematics, and the sciences to create the liberal arts we find in university programs around the world.

Until the beginning of the twentieth century in the United States, the idea of a "free person" studying these subjects made sense. Then from World War II onward, there was a shift to specialization and technical skills. The returning GIs wanted the skills to find and succeed in a job rather than an education that taught a person to think and reason. In general, such a movement tends to destroy a civilization from within, and we are watching the collapse, as it has been declining for the last forty to fifty years.

I'd like to make a case for you to fight back and take up arms by diving into the liberal arts. In the past, they have been taught so poorly that we forgot the "practicality" of poetry and art. But it's there. When I speak of the liberal arts, I mean the study and pursuit of knowledge through the arts, language, mathematics, science, philosophy, and history. We might debate some of these classifications and widen or narrow them, but in general, this captures the majority of what I mean. My space is limited to defend or develop a complete essay on the reasons behind my belief, but I would put forth some of the following practical reasons. In short, I believe that modern education is deficient in providing the tools to live as a "free person." Our schools teach through standardized tests, white papers, and absolute answers of the mechanical, where in contrast the liberal arts teach ambiguity, thought, creativity, and experimentation—the things that make us human.

However, to add some practical nature to this, here is some of the "why" to study the liberal arts.

The arts—architecture, music, literature, performing arts, and music—teach emotions. We love to study Emotional Intelligence. This is a psychology catchphrase popularized by counselors, trainers, and life coaches. Diving into the structure and emotion of the arts teaches the sublimity of feelings and emotions throughout the centuries and helps us realize our world as we live in it now.

Language is more than just being able to communicate to make money; it is a matter of thinking different thoughts. The reason we studied ancient Greek and Latin was that the thoughts we are capable of having in those languages shifted the mind, widened it to thoughts beyond a native language, and helped bring better understanding and context for a person's life. Through literature—prose and poetry—ideas transpire, and from there also emerges wider vocabulary, deeper concepts, and profounder thought.

Mathematics teaches us logic and reason. I'm the first to say that I'm not the most gifted in this area and I thank modern-day technology for spreadsheets and calculators on my iPhone. But in going through works like Euclid, I've seen theorems as beautiful as Bach cantatas and ideas as rich as any language. Buckminster Fuller's ideas on synergy still impact how we can work within curved space. Regardless of the numbers, the ideas and thoughts impact us all throughout our daily lives.

Science teaches us the power of the world around us, as grand as supernovas and new universes and as small as all the elements.

Philosophy asks us questions and we need to answer those questions. What is beauty? What is a good life? To change your world, change your philosophy. Diving into the works of Plato alone can change your world, but Nietzsche and Hegel ask questions of us that push us even further.

History, to my mind, is the parent of all the liberal arts. It provides the context where we can study art, science, and thought. We can paint a context of geography and geology, of economy and politics, and see how philosophy summarizes a society, and the arts predict the next age.

I'm not suggesting, however, that you stand on the sidelines and just read and study, though you can find the greatest women and men of the present and the past, of forgotten people throughout our planet. I would ask you to participate. It can be as simple as picking up an old guitar and starting to pick out a few chords. It could be sketching or drawing a vase of flowers. Yes, the chords may sound terrible and the drawing may look like that of a first grader, but everyone starts somewhere and it takes patience, practice, dedication, and effort to break through to an understanding of what the human is capable of.

I'm asking you to turn off the reruns of *Breaking Bad* or *Game of Thrones*—you've already seen it (some of us, myself included, more than once), and then dive into looking at what a "free person" is capable of. It may be a simple poem or two, learning to whistle, or the joys of cooking, but move from the animal—the receiving of facts, the watching television, the social media—into what makes each and every human on this planet who has lived and will live unique—creativity, thought, experimentation. Be worthy of your freedom or you will soon find yourself ensnared in the slavery of the masses. Build your *arête* of the body, mind, and spirit.

#SWEET SUCCESS: Go back and look at how history, mathematics, literature, the arts, and science all complete your world. How can the characters of the American Revolution help you build a sales team? Read the Declaration of Independence; do you see your own mission statement there? How does the thought process of Euclid's *Elements* affect your life? In what ways do Michelangelo's sculptures represent the sculpting of your life? Do you carry the same passion?

#SWEET SUCCESS: The easiest places to start to find the liberal arts are in one of these books:

- *Van Loon's Lives* by Hendrik Van Loon

- *Civilisation* by Kenneth Clark (the BBC television version is exceptional)

- *The Discoverers* by Daniel J. Boorstin

- *The Humanist Tradition in the West* by Alan Bullock

#SWEET SUCCESS: This week, take some time and do that art or craft you've always wanted to do. If you want to paint, but don't have any paints, take a pen and paper and start to draw. Set aside 10 to 30 minutes and just draw. If you want to play an instrument, visit a music shop and play. Ask if you can try the instrument. The point of the exercise is to create, out of you, something new. It could be physical, digital, or mental. You select and create.

#PICS

This exercise is good for a couple of reasons. First, we often forget where we come from and what led us to where we are. And second, the ability to have a vision is key in the creative development of who we can become.

In looking backward through our lives, we can see how where we are—sitting in traffic or riding a Ferris wheel or sitting in front of a monitor in an office on the 7th floor of a building—can be traced back, step by step, to a logical outcome.

The important point, though, is that although the decisions you made to get you where you are at this point may have made sense and had logical exactness at the time, you may find that some of the choices were haphazard, synchronous, or just downright lucky. Many events we say "happen for a reason" or luck fell into our hands, like happening to find a twenty-dollar bill on the street and then using it to buy a book that changes your life.

Or maybe the events may be less attractive, where you moved to a new city, started a company, and had success until a competitor emerged that could do the business electronically and made your service redundant. You had to sell your house, downsize, and now you are sitting in the unemployment office looking for a job, filling out forms, and sending out your resume.

In both cases, you're participating with the world. You're making decisions based on the facts that you know. Sometimes the outcomes are good, sometimes bad. The fact of the matter, though, is that you can and do make choices all the time, even when you don't make a choice, which is also making a choice. So when you are stuck, you know that it's time to make choices and move ahead. Yes, the outcome could be bad, but in all likelihood, if you don't do something, it could get worse. As Goethe writes, "Whatever you think you can do or believe you can do, begin it. Action has magic, grace and power in it."

The best way to see that path forward is to take a few minutes and think about where we have been and what were the choices and what we did well and what we can improve next time. The two questions I continually ask myself (and, to the chagrin of my sales team, ask them after every sales meeting) are: 1) What did you do well? 2) What can you do better next time? You may find these questions are beneficial. Feel free to ask other questions, as they will give you further insights.

The second point is that vision breeds creativity. There is certain potency in having a vision. The easiest vision that I have found is through the use of memory. Sometimes the memories are good and sometimes not so. We can reshape the memories and the stories and have them lead us to where we need to go in our lives. Then with this vision of the past, we are engrained with a certain wisdom that allows us to envision the future. We can create a vision and look at how each choice we make proceeding forward will impact what we do. William Boast often told me, "Who you are to be you are now being." It is very potent to look at ourselves and have a vision. The more we can build that vision and reconcile our past to agree with our present, the more we can build up the future and what we need to be.

#SWEET SUCCESS: Here is an enlightening exercise for you—find a childhood picture of yourself. Maybe it's a pic from your high school yearbook. Now look through and find a string of events that have hung together like pearls to lead from that moment in the photo to this moment in the present. For example, you may see yourself holding your mother's hand on the way to the lake to read a book. You may still love to read and find joy in reading to your children. This may carry on to your grandchildren. Or you may find a photo of you with an old boyfriend or girlfriend. How has knowing that person helped you? Have you made decisions that have led to other decisions that have led to other decisions that lead to this moment?

#CHOICE

Your whole life is based on the choices you make. In fact, you are a sum of all your choices. The bottom line is that you control your life. This may not be a popular belief. We like to blame something else. Maybe it's the weather's low barometric pressure causing us to feel tired. Perhaps the political climate. The boss is an ass. Whatever, we like excuses.

However, in truth, have you ever been happy on a rainy day? Have you ever done something wonderful or had a smile on a rainy day? Personally, one of the greatest things I do is go out on a long run in the quiet rain.

Granted, there are things in life that you cannot control. You read enough biographies in the world, and you find that Fate (with a capital "F" for a reason) or the cruelness of the world can take over from even the best people. Franklin D. Roosevelt lost the use of his legs. Beethoven couldn't hear. We still live in awe of Helen Keller. Viktor Frankl chose his life of freedom even locked in a concentration camp. The fact of the matter, no matter what life throws at us, is that we can choose.

One friend of mine, Leon Greenman, was swept away by the Nazis, along with his wife, son, mother, and fifty people from his village. They were all put to death except Leon and one other man.

After moving to three work camps, the war over, he found himself free. Rather than harboring hatred for the people who destroyed his family and life, he chose to move forward and educate the world. He spent the rest of his life working to educate people, like me, on the atrocities of war.

So let's admit some things are outside of our power of choice. We cannot select the weather, the traffic patterns, or what your boss will say when we get to work. Your son may throw up on your shoes, the window may crack from a stray rock thrown at it, and a glass of milk might spill. What you can control is your *reaction* to all these things. You can select if you feel angry or happy, if you sigh or cry or smile or laugh. Your reactions will greatly determine what happens next. A positive response brings positive reactions. A negative one, negative reactions.

On a daily basis, though, bombarded by choices, sometimes the simplest decisions trip us up. Look at the number of brands that line our grocery shelves, the choices of coffee at a coffee shop, all the shows on Netflix, and which social media to jump on.

Scientific research says that our ability to focus often determines our success. In order to push ahead through all the noise of choices, you need to learn to choose quickly and easily—to look at a menu and say, "Pow, I want the cobb salad!" and not second-guess yourself. This ability to control the choice of small things gives you the assuredness and confidence to select the bigger things.

The exercises this time will work on two things.

First, choosing to choose. You can select your reaction to what you cannot control. You can choose to make the reaction you wish and desire.

Second, strengthening your choice muscle.

#SWEET SUCCESS: Consciously choose to only react to what you can control and react the way you want. The Prime Minster or President did something you hated? You cannot control that. You can control your reaction—cease to complain or turn off the news or write a letter to your congressperson; make the effort.

Second, go out and make choices. Make some logically for a day. The next day, try some that are just on gut feeling or instinct or intuition (see the next section). Then write down the results.

Lastly, grab your commonplace and explore what the best choice you have ever made in your life was. How did you make that choice? Did you think through it logically or go on gut instinct? Go out today and make two choices—one based on logic, one on the gut. Which works better for you?

#INTUITION

Intuition comes from the Latin *intuitus*, meaning, "to look at, to contemplate." You can go through life taking in all the sensory information that bombards you every day—sights and sounds and feelings—and never really contemplate it. And then without notice, perhaps in the shower or while you're stuck in rush hour traffic, *bing!* A light goes off in your head and you have a *eureka* moment (*eureka* is Greek for "to find"). You have found an insight from all that sensory information that has bombarded you and the workings of your mind; all the parts came together, building the structure behind the scenes.

Sometimes, intuition is a hunch, an instinct, or first thought. Again, this comes from all these sensory images, and you may not have the *eureka* moment, but a small voice that guides you to proceed or not proceed. Socrates had a small voice that he called his "daemon," which guided him against mistakes.

Our minds are wired to see patterns. Sometimes there is a verbal reasoning that guides us into these patterns; at other times, it just "feels right."

Sometimes, when we are around people, we get a hunch, sense how they are feeling. We may not have any concrete evidence, may not see all the parts that fit into this conclusion, but our minds guide us.

Art, though often fashioned with rules of structure particular to themselves (think of a concerto form in music or a sonnet in poetry), dives deeply into the psyche, beyond words, and opens up an entire existence for someone else to witness and understand, even beyond words. Take the novels by John Steinbeck or Leo Tolstoy that throw themselves into scenes that can paint huge landscapes with words while being able to bring out emotions that have no words. Dvořák's "New World Symphony" or Debussy's "La Mer" do the same. Reading a poem by Emily Dickinson or Wallace Stevens or Gwendolyn Brooks, looking at a painting by Picasso or Matisse—some of their works hold the entire world and their beauty is beyond words, but intuitively we know they are "right."

Intuition is something that can be developed and practiced. By doing so, it provides you with greater insights and ideas. You may not always have all the facts and all the parts of a situation to proceed, so you have to go with the information at hand. Though the situation may feel ambiguous, you work to feel comfortable in this situation and take action.

The challenge occurs when trying to quiet the words and jabbering in our heads for a long enough time that we can actually be guided by our intuition. The time in the shower or driving a car is time when your mind is occupied and your intuition takes over, which is why many ideas happen at these times.

In your life, search for ways to concentrate and quiet the chatter in your mind and allow intuitive moments to occur. Many of the exercises in this book have attempted to help you do this. For me, this happens when I shower, when on a long run, if I meditate, and when I write. If I fail to do one of these things on a daily basis, my head fogs and the day is gray; decisions and intuition are more difficult to find.

#SWEET SUCCESS: Brainstorm twenty different things you can do to make your life more intuitive. Is it long walks in nature? Cooking? (The rhythm of stirring risotto or cutting a carrot is quieting.) Knitting? Drawing? Just sitting on a park bench for ten minutes and watching people pass by?

#SWEET SUCCESS: Take a day and make only decisions based on intuition. If you don't know what you should be doing at this moment, say to yourself, "What should I be doing at this moment?" and listen for the first answer. Then take steps toward doing whatever that command was, no matter how crazy. It may be a new project, skydiving, or painting. Start on it. As you continue, block out any words that are negative, but listen only to the small, quiet, calm voice that that guides—or in Socrates's case, prohibits. You will hear it say things like, "Good, go," or "Fantastic, that's enough, now stop." Sometimes it may even be abrupt. One friend said his voice told him to stop smoking by saying, "Stop being a jerk." He quit that day without any problem. Listen to your intuitive voice. As Albert Einstein said, "The only real valuable thing is intuition."

#TEACHING

Want to prove you know something? Want to master something quick? Want to do well in the world? Achieve world peace? End starvation?

Okay, living the old adage that "if you really want to learn something, teach" may not end with world peace, but it will certainly help you lock in what you know about a given subject. And you'll also help someone else as well!

When you teach, you can't just sit on your hands and passively learn. You need to get active, pay attention, engage with what you're learning. You are taking in new information that you will need to turn around and give to someone else.

One of my friends at Cambridge said most of the learning went on in the pubs after lectures. Not only did ale flow, but so did ideas and the uses of the ideas. In the classroom, the students absorbed the information, but in the pub they had to teach others, defend their ideas, debate their point of view.

As Richard Wilhelm points out in the *I Ching*:

Knowledge should be a refreshing and vitalizing force. It becomes so only through stimulating intercourse with congenial friends with whom one holds discussion and practices application of the truths of life. In this way learning becomes many-sided and takes on a cheerful lightness, whereas there is always something ponderous and one-sided about the learning of the self-taught.

The ability to teach shows us the beginner's mind. Not only have we learned something, we have to explain it. The process of breaking down the parts and showing the steps, of making something complex simple enough that someone else can learn, is a powerful tool.

#SWEET SUCCESS: Take out your commonplace. Where in your life can you teach?

#FAVORITE WEAPON

Miyamoto Musashi, the 16th-century Japanese swordfighter, said, "Never have a favorite weapon." If you continually fall back on a specific method or skill set over and over, you will grow predictable. You will be beaten.

Napoleon, crushing the Prussian army in the battles of Jena and Auerstedt, stood at the foot of the tomb of the legendary Prussian general Frederick the Great. Napoleon said to his generals, "Gentlemen, if this man were still alive I would not be here."

Napoleon alluded to the fact that the Prussian army had stagnated for a generation, drilling and mastering all the maneuvers that Frederick taught, but neglecting to learn and grow. The army grew predictable and Napoleon beat them.

Hannibal too routed the Romans at Lake Trasimene. Hannibal knew the Roman's lived (and died) by the motto, "death before retreat." Romans boundlessly charged ahead, while Hannibal anticipated and surround the soldiers and slaughtered them all to win a critical battle.

Do you have a favorite weapon? Do you do certain things the same way? Do you have a sacred cow? As Abbie Hoffman wrote, "Sacred cows make the best hamburgers."

To succeed, continually learn and improve. Remember, in business the competition ambitiously upgrades and changes. You need to take small steps, tweaking and refining each day. Train when others give up. Reading widely and deeply in a variety of fields, not just your specialization, cross-fertilizes new ideas and growth. Look to finish twelve books a year as a start. Beyond reading, listen to audio books. Then podcasts. And remember the importance of old-fashioned classroom learning. Take the time to continually upgrade old skills and learn new ones. Lastly, to put your learning on overdrive, find an executive coach to propel you to your potential.

#SWEET SUCCESS: Kill your sacred cows. Examine and initiate plans to improve and grow personally and professionally, intellectually, physically, and spiritually for the next twelve months; do one thing a month. Then execute constantly. As the adage goes, if you were traveling to the moon from Earth and changed the direction by a mere 1 percent, you'd miss the moon by 2,606 kilometers. Focusing on small changes, done consistently, brings continual renewal and accomplishment.

Before you tackle a task or project, image the outcome. Notice that the word here is *image* and not *imagine*. What you are looking for here is the ability to observe the image, hear, feel, and move around in the image. If you need to, take out a piece of paper and write down 20 questions about the project before you start. The questioning process drives you not to answers, but to images. For example, if you are creating a new product:

- Who will use this product? (See this person or persons. Image their looks—eye and hair color. Where are they? Image the whole scene as a movie. Pan in and out and around from different perspectives.)

- What does the person look like?

- What do they like? (Really look at them acting out their likes and dislikes, listening to their key phrases.)

- Where are they using it?

- What do they experience?

- Who sells them the product?

- Why do they buy it?

- How many will they buy in a lifetime?

- How will the product age?

- Over time, when will there be a follow-up?

- How many are sold? (Watch them selling, scanning, hearing the beeps.)

- Who manufactures them? (Observe the manufacturing process.)

- What is the perspective of the manufacturing process from the supervisor? Customer? Government?

- What is the attitude about your product?

- Why are you there?

- What other products work with your product? (Really see this image.)

- Who carries them?
- What is beautiful about your product?
- What are the colors and materials used?

Notice that this series of questions isn't for a "brainstorming" session and not for a committee. It is for an individual to create and then, from there, start moving forward and taking steps to create.

SERVE UP YOUR OWN HELPING OF #SWEET SUCCESS

Now it's your turn. We have gone through several ideas to build your *arête*. Now, in reference to the previous section, the best way to prove that you have learned something is to start teaching. The first person to start teaching is you. And then from there, you can start introducing these ideas to your family, friends, and places you work.

Start with a list of eighteen items for body, eighteen for mind, and eighteen for spirit. That gives you one item to add each week for a year. Now, take action on it. Some may work out and some may completely suck, but that's okay. The point is to live life in all its colors. If you stay in the same rut every day, you will soon be the rut. Create your own list and then get to work playing! Having gone through all the sections, you have the tools to create, think, study, observe, relax, design, and celebrate life and develop your *arête*.

Here's to you making your life a *sweet success*!

#SWEET SUCCESS BOOKS

Mortimer J. Adler, *How to Read a Book*
If you're looking for a place to start reading, this is it. A powerhouse on comprehension across the humanities and an awesome reading list.

Aristotle, *On Poetics (De poetica)*
Still the classic on aesthetic beauty.

Daniel J. Boorstin, *The Americans*
Boorstin makes history entertaining and fun! This three-volume set is the most insightful book on American history I've found.

Daniel J. Boorstin, *The Creators*
A powerhouse on the greatest artists to live.

Daniel J. Boorstin, *The Discoverers*
One of my favorite books on history. Just all kinds of interesting stories, such as how time was discovered.

William Boast and Benjamin Martin, *Masters of Change*
For business and life, look to the "who to" rather than the "how to" to master change—change which is normal.

Ray Bradbury, *The Martian Chronicles*
Insightful into how we look at our own species.

Van Wick Brooks, *The Flowering of New England, 1815–1865*
Brooks lived just after this renaissance and flourishing of U.S. thought and writing. Superb writing.

Van Wick Brooks, *New England Indian Summer, 1865–1915*
The second volume to Flowering.

Van Wick Brooks, *The Times of Melville and Whitman*
The flowering heads to New York.

Van Wick Brooks, *The World of Washington Irving*
The genesis of American writing.

Julia Cameron, *The Artist's Way*
A powerhouse program to creating more creativity in your life.

Julia Cameron, *The Right to Write*
My favorite book on writing guidance.

Julia Cameron, *Vein of Gold*
I like this even better than *The Artist's Way*.

Joseph Campbell, *The Hero with a Thousand Faces*
Simply the best in creating a heroic life and story.

Joseph Campbell, *The Power of Myth*
I recommend the video as you can see how animated and passionate Campbell is. Helps flesh out the ideas from Campbell's other works—all of which are fantastic.

Steve Chandler, *100 Ways to Motivate Yourself*
Simple ways to motivate yourself.

Kenneth Clark, *Civilization: A Personal View*
One of the greatest books on humanism. As mentioned, the BBC series is exceptional.

Kenneth Clark, *Leonardo da Vinci*
Probably the best biography on the legend.

John Dewey, *Art as Experience*
One of my favorite philosophies. Practical and applicable to life.

Will Durant, *The Story of Civilization*
Eleven volumes that changed my life.

Will Durant, *The Story of Philosophy*
The classic of understanding Western philosophy.

Betty Edwards, *Drawing on the Right Side of the Brain*
I used to screw up drawing stick figures and had terrible art teachers in school. A summer with Edwards's book opened up the world of seeing and art.

Ralph Waldo Emerson, *The Essential Writings of Ralph Waldo Emerson*
A pragmatic and wise transcendentalist.

R. Buckminster Fuller, *Synergetics: Explorations in the Geometry of Thinking*
Okay, a tough read, but the concepts are mind blowing.

Natalie Goldberg, *Writing Down the Bones*
Another good companion if you would like to write.

Natalie Goldberg, *Wild Mind*

Joanna Sayago Golub, *The Runner's World Cookbook*
Some solid recipes in here! Highly recommend the barbecue pulled pork. So easy to make and delicious.

Paul Halpern, *Einstein's Dice and Schrödinger's Cat: How Two Great Minds Battled Quantum Randomness to Create a Unified Theory of Physics*
A double biography of two of the greatest scientists of the twentieth century.

Roger Housden, *Ten Poems to Change Your Life*
Poetry that can change your life.

Edward Hirsch, *How to Read a Poem and Fall in Love with Poetry*
How poetry should be taught.

Ben Hunt-Davis, *Will It Make the Boat Go Faster*
A bit of sport applied to business skills.

James Loehr, *The New Toughness Training for Sports*
Energy management, not time management.

Christopher McDougall, *Born to Run*
Highly inspiring and insightful.

Jamie Oliver, *Jamie's 30-Minute Meals*
Oliver is a hero of the cooking world and revolutionized how I cook. Like playing piano with two hands rather than just one.

Plato, *The Works*
This isn't to give you philosophical answers, but only questions. Great questions should inspire you.

Plutarch, *The Lives of the Noble Grecians and Romans*
If you're looking for the one book that can help you build character, look no further.

Gabriele Lusser Rico, *Writing the Natural Way*
Like Betty Edwards's book for writing. Great for brainstorming ideas.

David Sedaris, *Me Talk Pretty One Day*
I like Sedaris's honesty and humor, with a tinge of sarcasm.

William Strunk, Jr. and **E.B. White**, *The Elements of Style*
If you write anything in English, and it seems we all write emails, read this.

Hendrik Willem Van Loon, *Van Loon's Lives*
The most wonderful way to learn history is to invite historical characters over for dinner.

Hendrik Willem Van Loon, *The Arts*
An encyclopedic history of all the arts.

Hendrik Willem Van Loon, *The Story of Mankind*
A brief and accessible story of our little history on this planet. Written for his grandchildren.

Roger Von Oech, *A Whack on the Side of the Head: How You Can Be More Creative*
Generate more and more ideas!

Walt Whitman, *Leaves of Grass*
To love humans with such passion and inspiration.

Richard Wilhelm (Translator), *The I Ching or Book of Changes*
Inspiration, philosophy, insight. Never the same book twice. I recommend this translation along with the preface by Carl Jung.

#ABOUT THE AUTHOR

DAVID SWEET is an author, poet, entrepreneur, executive coach, and runaholic. In the Sweet Success series, his books include *Sweet Success*, *Sweet Sales*, and *Recruit!*. His poetry includes *Pop Rocks* and *Split Infinity Forward*. He lives in Tokyo with his wife, sons, fish, and running shoes. He can be contacted at david@barefootlunch.com and found at www.drdavidsweet.com.

www.ingramcontent.com/pod-product-compliance
Lightning Source LLC
Chambersburg PA
CBHW070143100426
42743CB00013B/2808